BALI LIVING
Innovative Tropical Design

GIANNI FRANCIONE *with* KIM INGLIS
photography by MASANO KAWANA

TUTTLE Publishing

Tokyo | Rutland, Vermont | Singapore

Published by Tuttle Publishing, an imprint of
Periplus Editions (HK) Ltd.

www.tuttlepublishing.com

ISBN: 978 0 8048 4926 5 Pb
ISBN: 978 0 7946 0567 4 Hc

Distributed by

North America, Latin America and Europe
Tuttle Publishing
364 Innovation Drive, North Clarendon,
VT 05759-9436 U.S.A.
Tel: 1 (802) 773-8930; Fax: 1 (802) 773-6993
info@tuttlepublishing.com
www.tuttlepublishing.com

Japan
Tuttle Publishing
Yaekari Building, 3rd Floor,
5-4-12 Osaki Shinagawa-ku,
Tokyo 141 0032
Tel: (81) 03 5437-0171; Fax: (81) 03 5437-0755
tuttle-sales@gol.com

Asia Pacific
Berkeley Books Pte Ltd
61 Tai Seng Avenue, #02-12,
Singapore 534167
Tel: (65) 6280 1330; Fax: (65) 6280 6290
inquiries@periplus.com.sg
www.periplus.com

Hc 11 10 09   5 4 3 2
Pb 20 19 18 17   5 4 3 2 1

Printed in China   1702RR

TUTTLE PUBLISHING® is a registered trademark
of Tuttle Publishing, a division of Periplus Editions
(HK) Ltd.

PAGE 1 The Javanese joglo, a pavilion-style
structure of great integrity, finds new life in a
garden estate in Bali.

PAGE 2 This modern holiday home, built in
a verdant rice field seting, employs a "floating"
wood shingle roof that stretches over the main
structure.

RIGHT An inspirational example of how ancient
wooden structures find new life in today's Bali.
This indoor/outdoor living pavilion retains the
building's original carved roof and old columns,
but is updated with modern lighting and low-
level seating in neutral colours.

OVERLEAF Even though the twin roofs attract
the eye first, it is the wonderfully fluid transition of indoor and outdoor spaces that makes
this house the epitome of modern tropical
living today.

contents

bali at the crossroads

Bali has been labelled many things—tropical paradise, island of the gods, an idyllic Shangri-la, and more—but never before have such words as "urban", "conurbation", "traffic-clogged" and "busy" seemed appropriate. Earlier writers have tended to wax lyrical about Bali's ruralism, its rice field landscapes, its "otherness". They've discussed its largely intact culture, its traditional architecture, mores and religious practices and its other-wordliness that makes such a refreshing contrast with much of the rest of the world.

Rarely has it been referred to in terms of building booms, urbanisation and pollution. Commercialism, maybe, but certainly not rampant consumerism.

That seems to be changing now. Many of the mangroves and rice fields have disappeared in the Denpasar, Sanur and Seminyak areas, being replaced by highways and buildings. Ubud is no longer a sleepy artists' colony; it sprawls ever outwards. And many of Bali's sacred spots around its ancient temples have seen large, commercial developments in recent years.

Before this all sounds too depressing, it should be noted that there are still plenty of spaces on the island that continue to follow a quiet rhythm away from the madding crowd, as it were. Kintamani's slopes are still cool, pine-scented and sweet; the volcanoes are largely untouched. Much of the island's interior is still jaw-droppingly beautiful with undulating rice terraces and the north, east and west coasts (if you travel far enough) are fairly undisturbed.

RIGHT Tropical transparency at its best: This holiday home is characterised by the copious use of glass for indoor/outdoor living, but the eye returns again and again to the two monolithic "walls" rising from the central pool. They anchor the surrounding structures with a striking, elemental originality.

But, developed and developing, it is. Two previous books, *Bali Modern* and
Bali Houses, looked at the changing face of Bali's increasingly international
architectural offerings, and, in many ways, this book continues the journey.
All the structures featured herein have been built post millennium, and all
represent to some degree the continuing modernist trend. Whether it is
encapsulated in a restaurant, a private villa, a mini-hotel, a club, a garden
extate or a residential home is irrelevant.

Yesterday's primitive thatched huts are increasingly being replaced by large
hotels, resorts, private villa estates and sophisticated homes that – in many
cases – would not be out of place in more urban surrounds. They employ a
certain sophistication in building techniques and materials, and the interiors
are more cosmopolitan or designer authentic than rice field ethnic. This is
undoubtedly a major attraction for the more discerning vacationer seeking
to rent a villa for a tropcial vacation.

Certainly, Bali leads the tropical market in exclusive private villa rentals, but
there is another market that is growing even faster: that of the smaller
"village" where a series of almost identical rental villas sits cheek by jowl on
a fairly small plot of land. Architecturally, these are often fairly "urban" in
style – and they cater to the growing market from both within Indonesia
and from other Asian nationals, such as Singaporeans, Malaysians, Koreans,
Chinese, Taiwanese and the like.

This market segment is, for the most part, represented by a fair number
of stereotyped and standardized units that are less "tropical" than their

predecessors. People are attracted to the idea of a relaxing long weekend or week in Bali, but they don't want to leave their creature comforts behind. Hence, the number of urban box-like residences that are architecturally less creative and more utilitarian in functionality continues to grow. Such homes are also characterised by an increasingly homogenized style of interior design that features furnishings from the must-have imported brands now available island-wide. The general look is more business-like, perhaps a little more in the style of Asian apartment living.

Whatever one thinks about this trend, and the types of architecture it is producing, the island still continues to conceive and construct some buildings that are architecturally innovative, forward-thinking and, indeed, beautiful. For the main part, this book showcases a selection of private residences, but there are also a few public places that merit inclusion. Each is different in style: some retain links with the early tropical forms so beloved of the traditionalists, while others tend to be cleaner, more pared down, even minimalist. There's also the retro look (harking back to the past but still firmly rooted in the present), the glass-and-steel metropolitan configuration, and the updated rustic trend.

For the most part, the silhouettes tend to be sleeker than those featured in the past. There's a new sharpness, especially in the commercial venues, that mirrors Bali's more mercantile outlook. As the island attracts more short-stay sophisticates and less long-term dream-seekers, the environs shift accordingly.

RIGHT Modern materials as well as fixtures and fittings from global brands are increasingly found in some of the island's newer homes. This bathroom in a private home is a case in point: The sanitary ware and glass is sleek, but the garden trellising, use of pebbles and wood, and the abundance of the exotic plantings root the room in a tropical milieu.

RIGHT A first for the island, this wedding chapel is an audacious structure in any environment. Its light steel and glass A-frame seemingly floats on a reflecting pool, while the building's overt transparency invites the surrounding tropicality in.

RIGHT The Bukit area, with its
scrubland topography, provides
a suitably neutral environment
in which to build a home that
has no Balinese features what-
soever. Taking inspiration from
Western modernists, the style of
architecture is "tropical" only
insofar as it is transparent, with
a suitably blurred boundary
between inside and out.

All the properties featured have been selected because of their architectural creativity and their un-hackneyed interior design schemes; they are the perfect repositories not only for the new wave of furniture, furnishings and artworks that continues to be developed and manufactured in Bali, but also for the international materials and brands that are now available. In addition, they are representative of the type of indoor-outdoor living we have come to associate with the island. It could be argued that they epitomise the true essence of tropical living.

Complementing their surrounds and inviting views of ocean, jungle or rice terrace inside, they are, without exception, built from natural, yet increasingly refined, materials and furnished with a cool eye. Even though they may be more complex than their earlier counterparts, they still allow Bali's environment to take centre stage.

In some ways, Bali is at a crossroads. On the one had, there is the demand for globalized, standardized products, on the other there is a group of tropical visionaries creating ever more artistic offerings. In this book, we focus on the latter, with a by no means exhaustive selection of buildings that is unified by a sense of creativity and a contemporary aesthetic. Luckily, despite the current commercial direction the island seems to be taking, Bali continues to produce "organic" and sensitive architecture that fully anchors buildings in their surrounds.

Writers can indeed use hyperbole when considering these constructions; perhaps the urbanization can be held at bay a little longer?

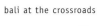

LEFT Sheltered beneath a tent-like wooden roof, this living room is simply furnished in neutral tones all the better to take in magnificent rice field views. Indeed, because the roof seemingly hovers, cross-ventilation is at a maximum and the feeling of really living within nature is amplified.

emerald shades and
serene spaces

Located in a compound in Canggu, these two villas are ideally situated close to the beach in a beautiful Balinese garden with mature trees and plantings. Although totally different in layout, design and atmosphere, they share a common architectural language, exemplified by the extensive use of old ironwood electricity poles as a structural and aesthetic element and the correspondence between the architecture and its surrounding landscape. Both villas take full advantage of the serene surrounds in which they find themselves.

Designed by Indonesian architect Yoka Sara of the firm Bale Legend, the villas employ both modern and traditional elements. Sara was aiming at a balanced composition, and this he has achieved with a strong interplay between curved and straight, horizontal and vertical, heavy and light. Named Emerald Sunset and Emerald River for obvious reasons, both villas are impressive additions to the Bali holiday rental scene.

Emerald Sunset is composed of three two-storey buildings linked by a second-floor terrace, which has fabulous sundowner views over the sea. The main volume sports a fresh architectural composition: old electricity poles and hollow steel beams form the basic structure which houses a downstairs living area and an upper relaxing corner. A slim curved metallic roof is the most eye-catching feature: it both insulates the building and seems to soar above it giving a general sense of agility and lightness.

This contrasts, yet complements, the other two structures that are rather more vernacular in form: an open dining pavilion and a building that houses the bedrooms. The latter is noteworthy for its use of double-height ironwood poles that support the roof and, in some cases, plunge down into the 20-metre-long (56 feet) curved swimming pool that hugs the side of the building. The pool is composed of lava stone and Indian slate tiles that change colour from emerald to sky blue depending on the time of day and the weather.

Emerald River, the second villa, is more traditional architecturally but is nonetheless stunning mainly because of the way its buildings have been incorporated around an "island" of mature trees and vegetation. Comprising four different two-storey buildings, linked on the second floor by a large terrace and connecting "bridges", it sports a curved pool with a dramatic concave overflow, attendant sinuous pavilion-style living and dining spaces and—again—the use of structural ironwood supports.

There is no doubt that guests are spoilt for choice as regards key locations in both villas: Where to lounge? A poolside pebble-washed terrace, an open-plan living room overlooking garden and rice field or a 25-sq-m Jacuzzi? What better dilemma to have when on holiday?

PREVIOUS PAGE At the entrance to the Emerald Estates, built for a French owner, Eric Lorin, and completed in 2005, all is calm, orderly and cool. The estate contains two villas; this building is the living pavilion of the one known as Emerald Sunset.

ABOVE Emerald Sunset is built in a u-shape: On the left is the modern living pavilion; at centre and right are two more traditional structures with wood shingled roofs. The smaller central one houses a dining area and the one on right the bedrooms.

RIGHT A double-storey pavilion with dramatic roof sits behind one of the garages at the entrance. The garage, marked by a decorative wooden grille on the curved wall and an inclined flying cover of metal, wood and plastic sheeting that plays with the bigger curved roofing above, is almost like an installation. The small planter box on left gives balance to the whole composition. The pavilion, itself, houses a downstairs living room and an upper relaxing area; built from ironwood poles and hollow steel beams with copious amounts of glass, its most striking feature is its slim curved metallic roof.

ABOVE The building that houses the bedrooms is hugged by a gently curving swimming pool that runs the length of the villa. The ironwood poles play both an architectural role (supporting the roof) and also freely interplay with the pool and deck below.

RIGHT An airy, open corridor leads to the entrance of Emerald River villa. A sequence of inclined wooden struts on metal supports carries a horizontal wood and metal ceiling; the poles dot the patterned pebble-washed floor and give character to the whole. A decorative Buddha-head painting at the far end gives a focal point to the gallery-style structure.

LEFT Water is a unifying and almost architectural element in the Emerald Estates. Here, the pool curves round the open-air dining pavilion and lounging deck, both simply furnished with items that weather well.

BELOW A swirling pebblewashed floor joins the entranceway with a living area that is arranged around a wonderful curved swimming pool. Casual, comfy modular furniture pieces in wood and rattan weave afford great views over the garden. A glass plate by Seiki Torige sits on one of the coffee tables.

BOTTOM The dramatic curved swimming pool of Emerald River divides the living pavilion from the more traditionally-inspired dining pavilion on the right. The two are connected by an overwater bridge and unified by prolific vegetation and the beautiful silhouette of a single palm tree rising out from the water.

ABOVE An all-wood rectangular pavilion houses the master bedroom and bathroom in Emerald River. Here, the décor is dominated by the colour red, with soft drapes, throws and cushions in scarlet silk and cotton.

BELOW The curved pool as seen during the daylight.

OPPOSITE TOP Night time bathing beneath the stars is one of the tropical dream seeker's secret indulgences. Here, the refined shape of an open-to-the-air bathtub cast in ivory terrazzo floats on a lawn of white pebble-washed concrete; it is surrounded by a textured slatted wooden screen. Terrazzo sinks for him and her are set adjacent in a covered section.

RIGHT A relaxing area on the first floor of the modernistic steel, glass and wooden pavilion has an airy, light feeling and almost 360-degree views out to the surrounding garden.

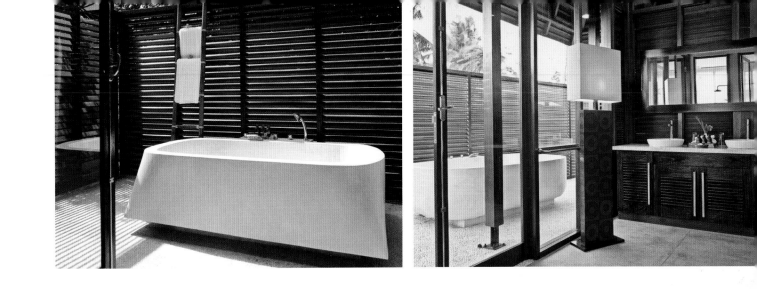

homage to the
Indonesian archipelago

Set amidst the curvilinear rice fields of Umalas in the Kerobokan area, this house, designed by a French couple, was built as "a tribute to Indonesian art and architecture". The idea was to produce something that is so particular to the locale that it couldn't possibly have been constructed anywhere else; it is also the repository of a vast collection of puppets, masks, primitive objects and folk art pieces collected by the couple over the past 20 years.

Comprising a variety of buildings dotted around a spacious 4,300-square-metre (5,140 sq-yard) plot, the architecture is vernacular in style. In addition to the main house, there is a Sumatran barn that doubles up as a poolside pavilion, a Javanese *joglo* that serves as a kitchen/dining area, a Balinese *balé gede* that is used as a relaxation unit, and an entire merchant's house from Aceh that is at least 150 years old. It now comprises spacious and spectacular guest quarters. All were bought, dismantled, shipped to the site and painstakingly reconstructed—along with a variety of doors, wooden panels and other salvaged architectural elements.

If this sounds somewhat anchored in the past—it isn't. All are set within a gently undulating expanse of lawn, and all have been reassembled with modern convenience in mind. Twenty-first century components include a curvy swimming pool, whirlpool, a modern kitchen with decent plumbing, a modish paint palette and some unusual materials. In addition, the art collections aren't displayed in glass cases; rather, they are placed in key strategic positions so as best to show off their unique characteristics.

"We did not intend to build a museum," assert the owners, "instead we wished that these beloved objects of ours would look alive and appealing in today's life." Careful space and décor planning sees a contemporary console matched with antique masks, a single carved door taking centre stage in a room, and colours combined in unusual and interesting ways. An example of this is a bathroom decorated specifically with green stone mosaic to match a pair of antique doors.

Elsewhere, the *joglo*'s white-washed and brown painted soaring roof results in a contemporary-style geometric pattern, while the colour palette of white, brown and green tones forms a delicate backdrop for a few key artworks.

Although many people have built ethnic-style homes in Bali's rice fields, not many have managed to produce estates with such panache. This one is simultaneously an enduring acknowledgement of Indonesia's peoples and heritage—and a wonderful family home.

PREVIOUS PAGE Guests love to sit semi-protected in the breezy ground-floor relaxation area beneath the merchant's house. Suspended rattan chairs are a take on Eero Aarnio's iconic bubble chair, while smaller stools have been fashioned from part of a Javanese *gamelan*. Other musical instruments include a drum and gong from Java, a green-painted zither and another part of the *gamelan* orchestra (with yellow flowers atop). The table in stone is from Sumba, while the pair of standing figures is from a Javanese advertising promo from the past.

LEFT The contemporary shape of the infinity-edged pool that looks over the lawn to the rice fields beyond echoes the shape of the land's contours. Decking in recycled teak and loungers in natural wood are unpolished, so look greyish and faded. An early 20th-century *Minangkabau* rice barn from Sumatra acts as a splendid poolside pavilion.

TOP A huge collection of *wayang golek* puppets resembles a "marching crowd" on a table in the living room.

ABOVE The master bedroom is a symphony of red and gold in Chinese Indonesian style. Rouge tones on the floor and walls were selected to match the antique Javanese bed. A variety of Sumatran, Chinese, Thai and Javanese trunks, tables and boxes form the furniture, while decorative items include a gold Burmese Buddha attendant, a lacquered red-and-gold wooden Buddha statue, a betel box (*tempat siri*), Javanese figurines and a mask from Java. In the corner, above an antique Javanese chair painted white, hangs a Burmese marionette. The overall effect with the soaring timber-and-thatch ceiling is overtly opulent.

LEFT A wicked-looking Javanese mask sits between a pair of Javanese figurines, all carved from wood.

OPPOSITE The interior of the antique *joglo*, a central Javanese structure, acts as the kitchen and dining room. Here the modern and the antique work well together: a country-style teak dining table and old Javanese bench sit comfortably with a contemporary side table housing an antique bird and masks from Java. Above is a soaring carved bird, also from Java; probably about 50 years old, it is a typical "folk art" piece. The side table was designed by Amir, a Sumatran antique dealer and craftsman, from an old block of teak wood. The Matisse-inspired painting follows the general colour scheme of taupe and olive.

LEFT Three traditional Balinese masks used in the *topeng* dance drama flank a mask from Cirebon (second from left); the latter would have been used in the oldest form of West Javanese dance that originated from the north coast.

BELOW Called Villa Artis, the main building is a simple, two-storey rectangular villa with an extended, protected verandah at ground level.

BOTTOM Bali has become famous for its open-air bathing options, so this Jacuzzi tub set in a deck of old teak boards from a hotel in Java with attendant lily pond is not such an unusual sight. What sets this one apart, however, is the attention to detail in the décor. On right sits a carved set of doors from Java, decorated with *wayang* figures; on left is a painting in the style of Matisse. The wooden figures by the tub are a pair of Javanese *loro blonyo*; protective figures, they are traditionally placed at the entrance of homes both as guardians and to welcome guests.

RIGHT Exterior view of the merchant's house from Aceh. It has a bedroom on the first floor and an open-air living area at ground level. Beautiful carved latticework and restored shutters ensure the upper level is well ventilated, while sturdy eaves protect the ground floor from sun and rain.

following the lay of the land

Built in 2004 as guest quarters for the home featured on pages 136–147, the form of this two bedroom home is dictated almost entirely by the shape of the land within which it snuggles. Sandwiched on one side by an access road and on another by a steep gorge, the house is almost in-built into the land. "The challenge was to make the house disappear from the driveway while totally integrating it into the tropical scenario," explains a spokesperson for GM Architects. This is fully realized, as it is only the singular shape of its two roofs that alerts passers-by of its existence.

The brief was for something "cute and different", and the architects accomplished this mainly through the two curved roofs that resemble the upside-down keel of a boat. The larger one is 22 metres (72 feet) long and both were constructed, pre-assembled at a workshop elsewhere in Bali, then cut into sections and reassembled on site. This was achieved by Tropical Buildings, a company that specializes in building stand-alone structures that can be packed and re-assembled in a different location at a different date.

The house comprises two buildings, a smaller one with a single bedroom and bathroom, and a larger main one, with living/dining quarters and one further bedroom. They are interconnected by a sequence of curved surfaces—walls, pools, decks, paths—that follow the natural contours of the land as it drops dramatically down to the river. These also help to fully integrate the home into the surrounding landscape and vegetation.

Needless to say, it isn't only the roofs that give this house character and substance. Certainly they offer an internal feeling of protection, as well as excellent natural ventilation, but there are other features of note. The use of materials—wood, natural stone (*paras* and *palimanan*)—and furniture crafted from shells, bones and coconut shards gives the house an earthy, organic quality suitable for indoor/outdoor tropical living. Of particular note is the open-plan living and dining areas: Situated over two levels with open access to deck and pool, the entire space is a pleasing mix of curved and perpendicular volumes, hard and soft surfaces, and light and dark shades.

If one were to view the home from an aerial perspective, the two volumes would look a little like two turtles crouching down into the surrounding vegetation. But when one is at ground level, all is airy, light, breezy and natural—and the surrounding trees, grasses, water plants and ornamentals are not merely surroundings. They are part of the entire whole.

LEFT The "front" of the main triangular building somewhat resembles a ship's prow. With a small garden and lily pond around, it is clad in grey *paras* stone to support the beautiful curved "flying" roof.

RIGHT Precision cutting, curvy shapes and a natural flair for organics such as coconut, bone and penshell result in some beautifully crafted decorative pieces from the atelier of Etienne de Souza.

LEFT The open-plan living room, wrapped by a soaring timber roof propped by a large V-shaped support, leads out to a *palimanan* stone deck on right and has a raised dining space behind, which opens up to another upper wooden decked terrace outside. A teakwood sculpture by Yasukazu Nishihata for Nakara complements teakwood flooring and a décor theme of organics.

ABOVE Wood decking, lawn, water and pebblewash and terrazzo are only some of the surfaces used in this entirely natural home.

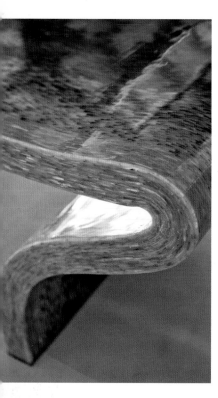

ABOVE Elegent detail of a long bench made from Tahiti mother-of-pearl by Etienne De Souza.

RIGHT The compact upper dining area features some furniture designed by Etienne De Souza from natural materials: of particular note is the square *grillage* table in bone-and-shell strips with legs in metal and resin with matching chairs in the foreground. Artworks are in keeping with the general organic theme—a painting by Peter Dittmar and a triangular teakwood art-piece from Ideas. The floor is composed of ivory *palimanan* to distinguish it from the teakwood section below (seen here on far right).

OPPOSITE The open-plan living area, with warm teakwood floor, features a low square sofa and coffee table constructed from bone shards; the camel-toned upholstery is in suede. The duo complement the coconut and penshell tray on the coffee table and the standing lamps in bone and shell. All were designed by Etienne De Souza.

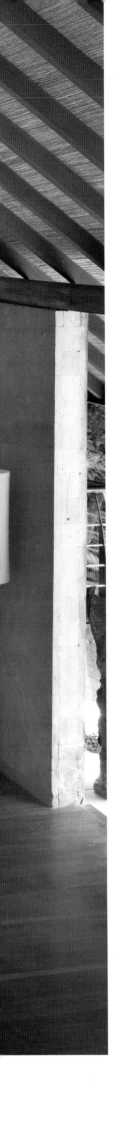

LEFT and ABOVE Precision cutting, curvy shapes and a natural flair for organics such as coconut, bone and penshell result in some beautifully crafted decorative pieces from the atelier of Etienne De Souza. They work well in this airy, organic-themed home. Above left shows some art stools in the foreground and a pair of "botero" vases in bone and penshell stripes; above right details the bone and shell star pattern of the coffee table.

BELOW The entrance to the villa is via a curved pathway that leads off the main access road. Two similarly-shaped curved shingled roofs shield both buildings: On the right is the master bedroom and bathroom, while, on the left, the somewhat larger volume houses the living and dining areas, the kitchen and another bedroom.

frangipani
frame house

PREVIOUS PAGE The modernist villa compound of this Indonesian businessman is dominated by a metal framework "roof" that stretches over the largest building. Both practical and aesthetic, it is composed from *ulin* wood and steel. The compound itself is imaginatively constructed over a number of different levels, using asymmetry as an overriding motif. Architect, Andra Matin, describes this as a "non-linear spatial experience, both horizontally and vertically". On left, a sculptural wooden teak root emerges from a reflecting pool; it goes some way to balancing the presence of the imposing, inclined frangipani tree in the middle of the compound.

LEFT The open-air living area in the double-height building is characterized by low-level tables in teak and simple *merbau* wood couches, designed to the owner's specification. Lime-green and beige cushions with a tree motif and purple upholstery offset a large modern painting by Indonesian artist Yuswantoro Adi.

RIGHT The two-storey building is open air below and enclosed above.

The frangipani tree (*Plumeria* sp), ubiquitous in the tropics, is planted extensively in Bali because of its sweet scent, interesting shape and for its cultural and religious significance. The blooms are frequently used in an assortment of decorative and ceremonial purposes. On this Seminyak site, a number of old frangipani trees, leaning in various contorted directions, cast their pristine flowers on the grass and their shade over swathes of lawn. They also serve as the inspiration for the design of the single outstanding architectural statement in this compound—an audacious steel roof framework.

It's the most eye-catching feature here—and not only because of its size and shape. Projecting over the entire mass of the only double-storey building in the compound, it seems to have a life of its own. "The framework derives its shape from the branches of the frangipani," explains Jakarta-based architect Andra Matin. "Creeping vertically and hovering horizontally over the concrete roof deck, it is extremely expressive." Consisting of steelwork clad in wood, it is both artistic and functional: it makes a strong sculptural statement and shields the flat concrete roof from direct heat and tropical rain.

Beneath its intricate webbing is a two-storey structure that stretches in an east-west alignment. The ground floor, entirely open to the elements, houses a living, dining and pantry area, while above are two children's bedrooms. According to Matin, the building is inspired by the traditional Asian stilt house where lower levels are open to the elements and enclosure is only made at the upper levels. Throughout the day, the living quarters benefit from cross breezes, ample sunlight and a seamless connection to the surrounding gardens.

The second structure, lying adjacent with only one storey, houses the master bedroom and bathroom. The architect originally intended to echo the frangipani theme with patterning on its outer perimeter wall, but this plan was abandoned after extensive discussion with the owner. Instead, the building found life as a simple glass-and-wood rectangle, with a flat roof and access to garden and pool. A third unit, located at the entrance, houses the utilities and, because of its size, effectively blocks off the sun's western rays from penetrating the central court. Thus, the entire compound is cool and fresh day long.

This villa, built for Indonesian businessman Mr Joelianto Noegroho, is an innovative example of how age-old forms can be transformed into something seemingly new and modern. Taking inspiration from both its immediate surrounds and vernacular structures, the architect has built a tropical-modern home deeply rooted in its milieu. And, in keeping with traditional Balinese architecture, a perimeter wall encircles the entire compound.

ABOVE The dining area is a study in simplicity with sturdy table and benches and a further low bench running the length of a wall clad in teakwood strips. A stainless-steel sink unit has been thoughtfully inserted into the table.

RIGHT Comprising a higher level lap pool and a smaller paddling area below, the villa pool is composed from *sukabumi* stone and sits in an *ulin* wood rectangular "carpet". In the background at centre is a relaxation area, also made from *ulin* wood. The pool's main rectangular volume connects to the relaxation area on one side and the master bedroom opposite; near the deck area the main volume overflows into a lower triangular pool.

OPPOSITE This angle on the low-level seating area gives a good view of the steel roof hovering horizontally over the entire space.

ABOVE The owner's bedroom and bathroom are housed in a single-storey unit that is accessed from the garden via solid unpolished terrazzo staircase with *ulin* wood treads. Completely vertically glazed, creepers cascade down from the roof softening the rigidity of the glass-and-steel structure.

BELOW The double-height structure with concrete pillars or "stilts" is entirely open-air on the ground level, yet sheathed in the strong webbed framework "roof". From here the view is down to the bedroom and bathroom.

ABOVE A wooden slatted roof, terrazzo and *ulin* wood floor and extensive use of glass give the master bathroom almost total transparency, highlighting the bathing-in-nature experience. A central island surrounded by water houses both shower and bathtub. The level of the floor is intentionally raised 750 mm (30 inches) from the ground level to signify its separation from the master bedroom.

RIGHT A low level Japanese-style bed gives a wood-on-wood effect in the simple bedroom.

tropical urban retreat

PREVIOUS PAGE The open-to-the-elements relaxation area positioned by the cooling pool is furnished with items that weather well. The attractive "wave double daybed" from Deefusion is made from woven *abaca* strips, while the floor lamps on left (called *pierres lumineuses*) are by Andre Cazenave Atelier. Even though they look like stones, they are in fact composed from polyester glass fiber lined with marble powder and are available from French firm Roland Jamois. The "uoval" table on right and the opened "standing uovation" lamp on the console aside it are designed and produced by the house's architect Valentina Audrito to further the ovoid theme flowing through from the dining room.

LEFT The dining area fronts a kitchen that is finished in black painted polished concrete (on left) and is separated from the living area by a black console (on right). The table with rattan fibre mattress is circled by "three-minute-boil" stools designed and produced by Audrito. Above are pendant silk cocoon and steel lamps designed by Angus Hutcheson in the "full moon" range from Bangkok-based firm Ango. A fruit basket by Cocoon and white-painted bamboo ceiling panel work well with the fibrous-covered bench; the floor is made from polished grey concrete.

ABOVE A balance of planes and volumes and a monochrome scheme is achieved in one of the en-suite bathrooms on the ground floor. A rotund basin in stainless steel sits on a thin steel cable suspended white counter; a bench separates it from the shower at back.

TOP RIGHT This handsome hand-made ceramic basin is from Gaya Fusion Ceramics; its dark colour contrasts with the wonderful soft light filtering in from louvers behind.

Rapid, often unplanned, development in the popular Seminyak area has resulted in poor infrastructure and over-crowding. Nowadays, many of the plots for villas and boutique hotel developments are small and often overlooked by neighbours. This house, built for an Italian jewellery designer by 35-year-old architect Valentina Audrito, was no exception.

With only 300 square metres (3,230 sq-ft) to play with, and a brief of two guest bedrooms with en-suite bathrooms on the ground floor and a master bedroom with en-suite bathroom above, the design proved a challenge. "We had a very small plot in a dense residential area," explains Audrito, " so, to maximise on space, I decided to keep the whole plan very simple." The result is a compact, two-storey tropical-urban home with clean lines and a minimalist white, grey and black colour palette.

The ground floor was designed so that the various rooms are not defined strictly by their function. An open-plan area that spreads out to the pool interplays with the two bedrooms that can also be used as living areas if the need arises. Similarly, the dining and living areas may be switched about at will. To lighten the slightly heavy, predominantly concrete structure, all vertical partitions (with the exception of the back facing the neighbours) employ wooden louvers so as to allow as much natural light as possible to filter in from all sides. Further softening comes in the form of rounded corners in all the walls: "This gives softness to the imposing lines of the structure and is also a tribute to the Mediterranean architecture that is both my and my client's heritage," explains Audrito.

Upstairs, the master bedroom has been treated like a loft where all elements merge together. This enabled Audrito to compress the room (while still giving it generous space) and clad it with terraces on three sides. These give privacy, while inviting the outside in. Similarly, the interaction between the bed, the bathtub, the shower, the sink area and the writing table gives the space a playful and fun feel.

This element of playfulness is furthered by a variety of the furniture pieces that were custom-crafted by Audrito: These come in the form of organic, ovoid shapes in primary colours and contrast with simple surfaces of white-painted *bengkerai* wood, polished concrete and white pebblewash. They also allow the architect to provide her client with the light-hearted space she desired in which to entertain.

ABOVE An aerial view of the entire house clearly showing the wrap-around verandah on the upper floor and the open-plan arrangement of space below.

RIGHT The entrance to the home is fresh with geometric shapes and forms. All external walls are painted in white rough plaster but softened by rounded edges wherever possible. This rounding off is echoed in the walkway stones set in an emerald lawn. The pool is the only feature that employs squared edges.

OPPOSITE TOP One side of the master bedroom features a black wash-basin and built-in surround along with a low writing table and "yolk" stool designed and produced by Audrito. The imaginative pendant light is constructed using a sari wrapped around glass.

OPPOSITE BOTTOM FAR LEFT The loft-style master bedroom combines bath, shower, basin and bed in an open-plan permutation that is lit from three sides by soft louvered natural lighting. The bed is covered in Indian sari textiles that beautifully match a dramatic red-and-grey painting by Filippo Sciascia. Adding a retro feel, in the foreground on left, is an iconic '70s sofa – "lips" by Studio 65.

OPPOSITE BOTTOM LEFT A black-coloured cement bathtub inserted in white-painted *bengkerai* wooden boards is placed directly behind the bed. Spherical ceramic hanging lamps are designed and made by the ceramics arm of Gaya Fusion.

home in the hills

PREVIOUS PAGE The home's infinity-edged pool in *sukabumi* green stone echoes the shape of the rice terraces below and also wraps around the house. A walk-way of free-form fossilised ivory stones connects two wooden decks and leads to the dining and kitchen quarters. Abundant landscaping of palms and white bougainvillea is contained within a black curved lava stone wall, while white frangipani trees throw shade and patterns on pool and deck below.

LEFT A path in pre-cast pebblewash leading to the house entrance is bordered by curved planter boxes in *paras Kerobokan* soft stone on the right and a water channel in the same stone on the left. The clad-in-Indian-stone roof of the dining and kitchen areas is visible on right, while in the background stands the profile of the main shingled roof that wraps around the core of the house.

TOP The detached guest pavilion, composed from green Indian stone and *bengkerai* wood, has a roof that has been cut to allow an entrance to be inserted. On left is a lily pond, while on right and behind is an expanse of untouched tropical vegetation.

The owners of this property were primarily looking for space to holiday with their children in natural surrounds without constraints. This was their major concern when briefing GM Architects on their future home in Tabanan, north of Tanah Lot. "We decided on a dreamy rice field setting as opposed to a smaller beachfront location, because we wanted space—a commodity that will become rare in the future," explains the Hong Kong-based owner.

This, GM was able to accommodate—in spades. The house, which comprises a main central building and a detached guest pavilion, is located literally in the middle of nowhere. Situated on a gently sloping hill looking over an amazing amphitheatre of meandering rice fields and surrounded by tropical forest, it is secluded and serene. In the owner's words: "The project manages to encompass that feeling of space without being threatening. On the contrary, a strong feeling of intimacy and hospitality flows through the house and its surroundings."

The challenge, from the architects' point of view, was to design something in "such an idyllic untouched place without disrupting the balance of the tropical pre-existences too much". To try to minimize the impact of the buildings, they worked with curved shapes and lines in an attempt to attune architecture and landscaping with the surrounding undulating rice fields and hills. In fact, so successful is the result, the project becomes a tribute to Bali's famed rice terraces.

The main building is articulated with two different architectural elements inter-playing together: curved shingled roofs and flat volumes clad in stone. A main long central roof shelters the entrance and living areas, while a second smaller roof covers the master bedroom; these are countered by flat roofs (elongated and round) covering the dining/kitchen quarters and the children's bedrooms. It is almost as if the house camouflages itself within its setting: the various volumes, along with the curvilinear lines of its pool and landscaping, blend with the soft volumes of the rice terraces all around.

Furthering the curviform theme, the guest quarters are rotund with an attached rectangular lily pond. Fashioned from green Indian stone and *bengkerai* wood, they have a flat roof that has been cut (like a piece of cake) to order to allow for the insertion of a wooden entrance. As with the main building, they seem to "disappear" into the surrounding hillside.

The owners had holidayed in houses designed by GM Architects before, so for them, the Italian architects were an obvious choice when it came to conceiving their own home. "We really enjoy the GM aesthetic, functionality and style, the extraordinary refined combination of warm and cold materials (stone walls with fine wooden lines) and the views that you have from every single corner of their houses," they note. When it came to their own home, they weren't disappointed.

ABOVE Surrounded by a lily pond, a relaxing area in the main home is sheathed by a roof that elegantly curves downwards so that it nearly touches the ground. The space is marked by vertical partitions (clad in ivory *palimanan* on right and grey andesite on left) which interplay with the black slate flooring and the all-wood surrounds. A coffee table crafted from a slim piece of teak resting on two black solid stones sits in front of a sofa in *abaca* strips and nylon from Deefusion; the bean-shaped standing lamps are also from Deefusion. The unusual hanging lamp in bamboo strips and shells is by Delighting, while, on right, is a mahogany root sculpture by Japanese artist Nishihata for Nakara.

LEFT A view of the sitting room and main roof from the front of the house shows the roof's beautifully curved shape.

RIGHT A change in materials, textures and colours in the flooring delineates the entrance to the house: whitish steps are replaced by black slates, while dark grey small pebbles are replaced by lighter, larger pebbles and, finally, teakwood planks. On the left is an all-wood waterfall inserted in andesite stone, while the wall next to it is in ivory Indian slate. A sculpture fashioned from a mahogany root is by Japanese artist Nishihata for Nakara.

ABOVE The living room, situated beneath the flying curved roof, employs a simple wood-and-stone palette. The curved volume on right houses the family's private quarter; it is clad in yellowish Indian stone, while, on the left, the powder room is in grey andesite patterned with horizontal stripes of teakwood. Between the two is a mahogany sculpture by Yasukazu Nishihata for Nakara called "Mugen". The sofa and bench in white woven raffia fibre from Deefusion sit adjacent a rectangular coffee table made from one piece of ebony supported on a teakwood central leg. The lamp in stratified glass and wood with a black shade (on the right) is from Marc Lé .

RIGHT A view from the guest pavilion shows the elegantly curved shingle roof of the master bedroom with triangular suspended wooden terrace. Plantings consist of palms and coconut trees.

LEFT The living area is positioned so as to take in spectacular rice terrace vistas, as the curved roof, propped by a V-shaped structural support, directs all eyes towards the panorama outside. On right is a sculpture in glass and wood by Japanese glass artist Seike Torige, while the two standing lamps in white-washed finished coconut wood at back are by DeLighting.

BELOW The lowest part of the relaxing area offers partial views of rice terraces and the curved volume of the dining area.

LEFT The master bathroom sports a handmade "floating" bathtub and sinks in teakwood set in a floor of black Indian tiles. In the background is a coloured glass sculpture by Seiki Torige.

BELOW LEFT to RIGHT Materials are key in the work of GM Architects: here we see close-ups of the roughly fashioned stepping stones between the two pool decks, the tiered glass support of the Torige sculpture and local pebbles under water in the pool overflow channel.

OPPOSITE BOTTOM The quintessential Balinese landscape with its undulating rice fields following the contours of the land.

RIGHT Rectangular volumes of different stone contrast with the curved line of the shingle roof.

BELOW A view of the home from the top of the hill behind shows how the buildings blend into the hillside and merge with the surrounding rice terraces. The soft curved main wooden roof floating over the living area plays with the sharp elongated flat stone-clad layer of the dining and kitchen quarters on right and the curvilinear pool below. The landscaping follows similar wavy lines.

OVERLEAF Drama by dark: Early evenings at the rice field home are particularly tranquil, with only the sounds of frogs interrupting the stillness of the night.

an exercise
in restraint

The home of designer Alessandro Landi is unabashedly modern, with a simple layout that embraces open-plan living. In order to optimize spectacular views over its remote southern coastal location on the Bukit peninsula, floor-to-ceiling glazing is liberally used. To further the feeling of living with nature, the apparent lightness of the structure is countered by an exuberant use of rough, unfinished textures—from slate and stone masonry to granite and bamboo flooring. The overall result is an international-style, contemporary home with no rice field in sight.

Inspiration for the four-bedroom house came from the work of mid-century modernist architects such as Richard Neutra, John Lautner and Pierre Koenig. "These architects advocated that architecture should serve as a mediating force between man and nature," explains Landi. "Their work epitomized the essential joys of modern living: sun, space, greenery." Landi was keen to embrace these ideals in his own home, as the surrounding terrain is somewhat unusual for Bali being rather drier and less "jungly" than in other areas. It lends itself to a more cosmopolitan style.

Unlike many homes in Bali, there is little reference to Indonesian culture either inside or out. The entrance is a particular case in point. Access from the carport is via a wide staircase of flamed granite, flanked on both sides by bright yellow plantings, a smooth concrete garage wall and a grille of vertical *bengkerai* wooden slats in different widths and heights. This international atmosphere is furthered once you enter the house: interiors represent a departure from the norm in Bali where Indonesian accents tend to predominate.

The palette of the interior echoes that of the exterior: Several shades of grey are utilized from a light hue on the ceiling, columns and floor, to a silvery Indian slate wall that delineates private and public areas, and dark blueish-grey external walls. Charcoal sofas and dining chairs, as well as black glass bar and kitchen cabinets, comprise the main elements in the open-plan living/dining/bar/kitchen space; these are juxtaposed with calculated splashes of colour—a bright red chaise longue on the deck, a crimson rug in the living area, red-and-chrome bar stools and a triangular awning on the deck.

All around are views of the garden with minimalist landscaping, a narrow lap pool lined with irregular blocks of green *sukabumi* stone, and the Bukit scrubland. As an exercise in restraint, the house is perhaps unparalleled in this book.

PREVIOUS PAGE An external view of the house as seen from the garden: The open-plan layout is accentuated by floor-to-ceiling glazing that blurs boundaries between the interior and the outside.

ABOVE Positioned so as to give expansive views of the garden and scrubland beyond, the open-plan interior is a symphony of grey tones with the odd splash of red.

RIGHT A long lap pool runs the length of the house. Surrounded by a deck and lawn edged by double rows of *Stipa gigantea* grass, it echoes the line of the house's long, precise roof. The roof itself is built from reinforced concrete with a five percent angle so as to allow rainwater to be collected via a large network of pipes and stored in a reservoir under the pool.

ABOVE and RIGHT The open plan interior features casual, yet modern, furniture pieces that work well with Indian slate walls and granite flooring. Planter boxes with geometric grasses sit alongside abstract paintings on glass by Landi. Using nitrocellulose paint and an array of mixed media, they are supported on volcanic stone blocks. An imposing Asmat war shield by Just Jen's in Seminyak is the only nod to Indonesian art. According to Landi, it has been left casually leaning against the living room wall "as if abandoned by a warrior at the end of a headhunting expedition". The glass-topped coffee table sits on top of rough blocks of wood.

BELOW The generous outdoor dining deck, shaded with a triangular awning, is flanked by a row of twin palms locally known as "Squirrel's tails".

ABOVE Indian slate and sandblasted glass are examples of the textures used in this modernist home. The flooring of flamed impala granite is smooth and clean.

LEFT The thoroughly modern entrance from the carport up to the home entrance is via a flamed granite staircase with dramatic yellow plantings. Scattered quartzite cobbles serve as punctuation marks, while textural appeal is to be found in the asymmetric *bengkerai* wooden "wall".

FAR LEFT Several yuccas and agaves, along with scattered stone "bedding", in a small garden at the entrance add their sculptural presence to the more abstract geometry of the house. Floor to ceiling glazing invites their presence inside into the kitchen too.

ABOVE At night, the garden comes alive even more than during daylight hours. When viewing it from the house (as here), the texture of barks and leaves are highlighted by subtle lighting effects.

BELOW This lit sculptural effect is highlighted on an upper staircase that leads to the entrance proper: Grey tones, concrete-and-glass and minimalist rows of agave predominate.

LEFT At night, concealed downlighting accentuates the rough hewn texture of the living room's untreated stone wall. The different heights and lengths of each individual piece are sharply delineated, illustrating how the masonry in this home is an important design element in itself.

BELOW Dramatic lighting both in and around the pool anchors the poolside deck to the open-plan interior of the house. A large round lifht from Lightcom adds drama on the deck.

cross-cultural hybrid

PREVIOUS PAGE The main living/
dining *joglo* as seen from the
front. Walls have been replaced
by glass for total transparency,
and views from the deck look
over the pool and rice paddy to
the ocean beyond.

LEFT A supremely comfortable living
space in the main living *joglo*
has been achieved with a restful
combination of new and old by
designers Jasmine Saunders-
Davies and Myriam Toussaint.
Composed entirely of recycled
teak, in furniture, floor and
structure, variety is introduced
with contrasting textures and
tones. The graphic lines of a
modernist stool on left are
juxtaposed with a primitive table
hewn from an antique Javanese
weaving table. While all the
furniture was made by Old Java,
the room is softened with white
cotton drapes and upholstery
and carpets from Disini that take
their tones and patterns from the
natural world.

BELOW The entrance to the main
living/dining *joglo* is via a walkway over a reflecting ornamental
pool. Limestone and lava rock
are used liberally in pathways,
pavings and poolscapes.

Traditional Javanese *joglo* houses are structures of soaring symmetry with a steeply pitched roofs that end in a blunt tip and flare out forming wide eaves that protect from tropical rain and sunshine. Having their roots in temple architecture, they are made from wood and often sport intricately carved ceilings, pillars and walls. Unfortunately, due to the rigours of climate and topography, many have fallen into disrepair.

It's all the more welcome, therefore, to find an estate on 1.5 hectares (3.7acres) of land on the clifftop above Selonding beach that is composed entirely of renovated *joglos*. Open for rental, the owners are Mark and Jasmine Saunders-Davies, a couple that also owns Old Java, a Java-based furniture manufacturer that specializes in reworking old teak. They started "collecting" dilapidated Javanese *joglos* some five years ago after they bought the land, with the hope of preserving these important historical structures. Gradually they formulated a plan to modernize them but keep them true to their architectural heritage.

To do this, they enlisted the help of Singaporean architect Cheong Yew Kwan, a designer well known for his interest in indigenous styles of architecture. Many of Cheong's previous projects display a deep respect for traditional forms, which he combines with a contemporary aesthetic that takes influences from both Asia and Europe. He is also committed to environmental preservation, another factor that swayed the owners in their choice. Their plan was to incorporate an eco-friendly approach in the project, something that has now been achieved. "The swimming pools use ionizers, not chemicals," explains Jasmine Saunders-Davies. "We use solar heating to heat the water in all bathrooms and have a computerized underground sprinkler system for the garden to minimize waste."

Cheong placed the *joglos* in a semi-circular arrangement so each has unobstructed ocean views: Because of their condition, they were all extensively re-engineered with concrete foundations and walls and wood shingles for roofing. However, the original pillars and carvings were left intact. Salvaged teakwood is used for flooring, doors and furniture, while the front panels have been replaced by floor-to-ceiling glass, in order to give them a lighter, more contemporary feel.

Khayangan Estate, today, is a noteworthy cross-cultural hybrid. It's a fine example of how architectural treasures can be picked from their national dustbin and turned into mainstream revenue earners. But it is also a little bit more: Taking its name from the Sanskrit word that roughly translates as "Seventh Heaven", Khayangan is thoroughly imbued with a palpable history. As Saunders-Davies says: "We have preserved the essence of these buildings, but at the same time made them more user-friendly."

ABOVE The living/dining *joglo* opens out on to a large terrace with an infinity-style swimming pool, lined with green *sukabumi* stone and faced on the outside with black lava stone; beyond are fabulous views of the ocean.

RIGHT *Joglos* tend to have ceilings that are beautifully carved in concentric, ever rising patterns. As they reach ever upwards towards the heavens, they become ever more elaborate.

LEFT Six-star service in historic surrounds: Khayangan Estate in Pecatu, Uluwatu, is a breathtaking rental estate where guests house, dine, bathe and sleep in painstakingly reworked Javanese *joglo* houses.

OVERLEAF Tall vases of tuberoses, long pillars and standing lamps, in conical and spherical shapes, from DeLighting prevent the ceiling from seeming too high in the main living/dining *joglo*.

ABOVE The dining area at one side of the main *joglo* is illuminated by standing and hanging lamps from local firm DeLighting; they cast a soft glow over the entire area.

RIGHT Natural materials are used for imaginative effect in a guest bedroom. A black bathtub sits in a frame of old teak; the fretwork wood panels, lit from behind, cast a romantic glow on the interior.

OPPOSITE A guest bedroom pavilions features furniture on the deck from Hishem Furniture; all the *joglos* are sited within view of the pool and with views over the ocean.

LEFT The Sultan Suite boasts a king-size bed inserted in the centre of this spectacular *joglo*, the ceiling of which is particularly fine. The floor is composed of large old teak planks, somewhat softened by an organic-patterned carpet from Disini. Wall lamps in swirling wrought-iron and glass from DeLighting are attached to the ancient pillars, casting a soft glow over the ancient structure.

ABOVE A free form solid stone washbasin sits on a massive teak plank counter in a guest bathroom.

ABOVE and RIGHT TOP The master bathroom sports both an interior and exterior section, divided by glass. The internal part is characterized by the extensive use of old wood: large teakwood planks comprise the flooring while a solid teak block forms a counter. The warm wood tones are matched with taupe on the walls and combined with a pleasant insert of white pebbles in front of the toilet and shower. An antique rustic bench and white cotton drapes add a decorative, rustic appeal. Outside, in a garden setting, sits a canopied bath on a block of black lava stone, a shower, private plunge pool and *balé*.

RIGHT BOTTOM Neutral shades of cream, white and taupe form the perfect backdrop for a guest bedroom, leaving the focus on the natural patina and carvings of the old wood. Bedside lights from DeLighting.

tropical
transparency

When the owners of Tra villa first visited Bali, they weren't particularly taken with the island. They found it a little busy, a little too commercialized for their taste. It was only once they had explored its heartland of jungle and rice field that they fell in love with it, and decided to build their tropical dream home. "We wanted to recreate the feeling of always being outside in the middle of the forest and rice fields," they say — and this vision has been fully realized at Tra.

Built in 2006 to 2007 in Canggu, the brief to the architect was "something unique, pure and simple but elegant, not 100 percent Balinese and not 100 percent European in style." This was achieved by designer Yoka Sara of Bale Legend with a modern, simple design that uses a combination of hollow steel, a composite aluminum material known as alucobond and plenty of glass. Ironwood columns salvaged from old electricity poles add character, while grey sandstone and *sukabumi* stone work well with polished concrete, terrazzo and pebblewash flooring. Combined with the restrained style of interior designer, Dominique Seguin, who liberally uses linens from her pristine store Disini, the overall effect is clean and easy on the eye.

The villa also has a transparency that allows the architecture to "appear yet disappear" in the words of designer Yoka Sara. "The villa is located in the middle of a rice field with a small river at the end of the land," he explains. "We oriented the villa towards the river, with the main level raised above the existing level of the paddy field. But when you are at the entrance, it looks sunken, thereby creating a new panorama — one where the architecture merges with nature."

This was furthered by the landscaper's choice of common plants from the surrounding natural landscape: king grass and pandanus on roof garden spaces, groves of banana trees drifting up from the jungle to the pool area, and tall stands of slim palms. "We always try to achieve a fusion of architecture and landscape design to create the ultimate living space," explains a spokesperson for Tropland, the landscapers in question. He goes on to note that such a space needs to be integrated into the surrounding landscape, made a part of it.

Another noteworthy feature at the villa is the construction of two tall "walls" that rise up from the middle of the pool. Clad in dark green *sukabumi* stone but appearing black as they are constantly covered in water, they're a dramatic addition to the poolscape. Their verticality both interplays with the horizontal planes around them and acts as an anchor to the entire architectural composition. Wherever you gaze in the compound, your eyes are continually drawn to them: iconic elements in a sunken, semi-hidden whole.

PREVIOUS PAGE Dramatic pool, garden and house lighting at night all contribute to the tropical transparency that is the main design feature of this home.

RIGHT The central part of the house contains the entrance and living/dining area: with maximum transparency, it is a fresh example of the contemporary-tropical villa. Interior stairs on the right lead up to the front entrance, while exterior stairs on left lead down to the pool. Old ironwood electricity pylons inserted in hollow steel tubes form the supports for the entire pavilion-style structure; an antique bench on the terrace gives a Javanese retro feeling.

TOP Access to the living/dining pavilion is via an elegant staircase from the front door. The dark grey tone of the walls frames the entrance and works dramatically with a pale polished concrete floor. Stark geometry is softened by the addition of sculptural palm tree trunks on either side.

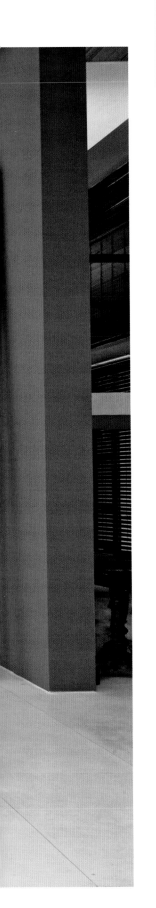

LEFT A contemporary modular sofa by Disini features a greyish washed wood base and stroped upholstery that echoes the staircase on right. The Javanese coffee table and dining table (in foreground) are antiques.

ABOVE Sitting adjacent the pool and at right angles to the main living pavilion is a structure housing two bedrooms and two bathrooms: all four volumes are slightly different from each other giving an unexpected impression of lightness and agility. A somewhat severe grey block not yet covered by green creepers encloses an open-to-the-sky bathtub. Here plantings were chosen for their fragrance: night jasmine, tropical magnolia trees or *cempaka* and frangipani (plumerias).

BELOW One of the villa's four bedrooms features a bed in grey washed *bengkerai* wood with linens and cushions from Disini. An antique ancestor wooden statue from Kalimantan is both protector and guardian.

BELOW A bathroom features a custom-crafted shower cubicle made from wood and glass. The walls, floor and sink are all in polished concrete in greyish tones.

RIGHT and FAR RIGHT An open to the elements shower on the pool deck is composed from a simple polished concrete wall and a giant wooden root that acts as a screen. The two different textures juxtapose beautifully with the dark vertical "walls" in the pool.

RIGHT Two slim sculptural "walls", clad in dark grey *sukabumi* stone, emerge from the Tra villa pool giving the whole compound a strong identity. Water exits from outlets at the top of these walls, providing a double purpose: aesthetic (the stone is always wet, black and shining) and utilitarian (they serve as water inlets for the pool).

indoor-outdoor Living

Designed by Italian GM Architects, this villa is one FROM a 22-villa complex in Seminyak called the Layar. In Indonesia, *layar* means "sail" and this aptly describes the single most iconic feature of the home—a distinctive sloping roof, made from natural ironwood shingles, that extends from almost ground level and interplays with horizontal and vertical planes and volumes. It draws the eye from whichever angle you look at the home.

This style of roof has been called GM Architects' signature, but the company is quick to point out that its work encapsulates much more. "We always look to create an organic type of architecture, one that is naturally connected to the environment," says a spokesperson. "Materials, textures, the finishing, the relationship between landscape and architecture—all are high on our agenda." Certainly in this villa, the connection between the different internal spaces and the exterior is fully explored: there are intimate protected areas, wide open-to-the-sky decks and other areas that merge the two. Adding different levels has provided a further dynamic.

Quality of materials is another hallmark: A variety of natural building substances—Indian slate, andesite stone, acid-finished unpolished marble and tropical *benkerai* wood—are all utilized with a deft hand. Soft and hard, curved and straight, fluid and geometric, all juxtapose to create a bold architectural statement, yet one that encapsulates easy tropical living. Whatever you think about Layar's highly original style, the home is user-friendly, compact and energy efficient. And the proximity of the pool and garden, with framed views, makes for a real indoor-outdoor tropical living experience.

In a bid to up the eco-friendly factor, the architects utilize natural light and ventilation wherever possible. Light and breezes enter freely in places where one angular roof seemingly hovers over another, or where walls and partitions are separated from the roof structure. In addition, the ceiling above the upper living area at the back of the house is composed of a series of wooden L-shaped beams connected with panes of glass; these invite different types of light to filter through into the interior. Similarly, spaces between deck and living area, front entrance and interior, kitchen and garden are left fully open, facilitating plentiful cross-cooling. The only enclosed spaces are the three bedrooms.

Over the years, GM Architects has carved a niche in Bali's architectural scene. Known for bold, modern forms, it's easy to gloss over their architects' respect for the local environment, their ability to re-work traditional Balinese forms, and their adherence to what is a typical Balinese tradition: living closely with nature. At Layar, these factors are key to the overall design.

ABOVE Characterized by its bold, geometric roof forms, this villa has all the ingredients for a cool modern tropical-living cocktail: water, garden, indoor-outdoor spaces and a strong, yet fluid, connection with the surrounding landscape.

OPPOSITE The curvilinear shape of the pool contrasts strikingly with the geometric forms of the villa roof. A triangular Jacuzzi sits adjacent a deck in *bengkerai* wood, on which modernist loungers from Hishem Furniture have been placed. The pool is tiled with *sukabumi* stone tiles in a gorgeous deep green shade.

ABOVE The main living area, wrapped by its seemingly hovering wood-shingle roofs, opens to the pool on left and leads to another higher-level lounging area (in background on right). The interiors are designed by Luca D'Alessandro, a Bali-based interior designer, who custom-crafted all the furniture in the villa. A sofa suite in white-washed rattan with charcoal upholstery, wooden coffee table and two standing lamps in metal work well with a collection of decorative lava stone panels on the wall. The cool floor is in unpolished marble finished with acid.

LEFT The transition from *bengkerai* wood decking to unpolished ivory marble flooring marks the entrance to the villa. The curved wall, on right, is clad in Indian slate.

OPPOSITE TOP A view from the living room out through the main entrance of the house. The curved wall (on left) and triangular wall (on right) play with the wooden structure of the roof to produce a dynamic architectural composition that defines the indoor-outdoor transition of the villa.

OPPOSITE BOTTOM Another exterior view shows the second poolside deck and the way one roof form slots over the other.

RIGHT The master bedroom is a cool combination of beige, taupe and cream with a white *palimanan* floor and leather-and-wood chaise lounge (just seen on left), armchair and bed in chocolate tones. A selection of local artefacts sits on the ledge behind.

TOP RIGHT A raised upper area with television, ideal for lounging, sits beneath a wood beam-and-glass ceiling and has access to the back terraced garden. A large coffee table composed of a giant wooden root and glass top takes centre stage, while two oversized sofas in midnight blue provide comfort seating. Painted wooden panels on the walls and two standing lamps in hemp were both designed by Luca D'Alessandro; another decorative details is the horse head on the back wall.

TOP LEFT Adjacent this upper sitting room is a utilitarian kitchen and serving hatch. Here, as elsewhere, the *parti* is open plan.

ABOVE To the right of the master bedroom is a slightly Japanese-inspired sitting area that looks out over the back garden—wood and glass combine here for symmetry, but also to allow the room to be air conditioned.

RIGHT A view of the entire house by night taken from the pool. The photograph clearly shows how, beneath high ceilings, the open-plan living areas are at the heart of the home. From them radiate the decks, pool and gardens, creating a fluid transition between indoor and outdoor.

a surfer's
dream home

This exclusive private retreat, built for an American businessman who has been working and surfing in Indonesia since the mid 1970s, encapsulates all that is close to a dedicated surfer's heart. It has fantastic ocean views over arguably two of the best surfing locations in Bali, Padang Padang and Suluban; it epitomises casual, indoor-outdoor living; and it has easy access to the waves.

Designed to a concept formulated by David Lombardi, the house is located on a bluff facing to the north west. It consists of a main central structure with a shingled, pitched roof flanked by two lighter, flat-roofed volumes housing bedrooms, a detached building with extra guestrooms, a carport and a swimming pool. "The intention was primarily to capture the view from the site and integrate the kitchen and living spaces while keeping the bedrooms private," explains Tim Watts, the owner. This has clearly been achieved.

The spacious living/dining area with attached kitchenette comprises a large loft-like space that is almost completely open plan. Built from ivory *palimanan* stone with cool terrazzo floors, it looks out to the garden, pool and ocean vistas beyond. The shape is slightly concave, so as best to view the waves, and it sports a seemingly floating roof that is supported by a series of old ironwood poles. With comfy furniture in organics and fresh breezes from the sea, there is little to disturb the equanimity of a surfer's mind.

It's a little unusual to find a carport in Bali, but it's a useful addition to any home on a rainy day. Another feature that gives this house a certain individuality is the perforated copper door at the main entrance. Fashioned by metal artist Pintor Sirait, it's really an artwork in itself. Using a central hinge, it is an example of how Bali lends itself to the bespoke market. Artisans, using many different media, can sculpt, paint or craft literally anything that a client envisages.

Over the years, Bali has seen its fair share of surfing aficionados attracted to the island's rich challenging southern coastline, cheap living, easy-going population and pleasant climate. Tim Watts is only one of a host of dedicated surfers who have come to view the island as their second home. When the trade winds are blowing in the right direction, the tides are right and the sun is out, this crowd keeps returning for more.

There's seemingly no satiation as far as these big blue rollers are concerned—and Watts' residence on the famed Bukit peninsula meets any surfer's requirements more than adequately. Laidback living meets California cool on Bali's coastline: what could better that?

ABOVE and PREVIOUS PAGE A slim lap pool, with an old driftwood diving board, separates the house from the ocean. Landscaping is minimal and natural with sea almond, palm and frangipani trees; sea almond are able to withstand salty sea breezes so are a sensible choice here.

LEFT Al-fresco dining at Watts' residence is always accompanied by garden and ocean views. The table, with glass top and intertwined rattan, wicker and steel base, is suitable for the outdoors. Chairs in *abaca*, nylon and mahogany are from Deefusion, as is the table. Sturdy salvaged ironwood electricity poles support the roof, while the floor is in hand-made terrazzo with sweet square-cut marble insertions.

ABOVE Tim Watts' mascot sits in the middle of the well-maintained lawn!

RIGHT A large loft-like space open to the garden and overlooking the ocean is the main focus of the home. Two vertical partition walls with round decorative windows flank the front door and help delineate space in the enormous area. In the foreground, linear sofas and coffee table in a dark brown weave ensure comfortable lounging, while the bamboo-and-rattan lamp casts illumination for reading. All are from Deefusion. On the other side of the main door is the compact kitchen/dining area: a simple teakwood counter with a built-in base divides the open kitchenette and the dining area. Behind the dining table and adjacent one of the bedroom doors, is an artwork in green glass by Seiki Torige.

RIGHT One of the bedrooms with teak-framed French doors looks out to a large stainless steel and polyurethane egg-shaped pillow installation sofa designed by Valentina Audrito. Behind, on the curvy deck fronting the pool, is a comfy lounging chair and coffee table in steel, nylon wire and polyethylene from Deefusion. Intended for the outdoors, it is extremely hardwearing.

LEFT Ducks, kept by farmers to keep rice fields free of pests (and also for the pot!), are playfully realized in a wooden procession on the lawn.

LEFT Tim Watts' oceanside residence is wonderfully open and airy. Living and lounging, eating and drinking takes place in the central portion beneath a gently pitched shingled roof. The two bedroom wings on either side add slenderness, while the disconnection between the roof and the walls below gives character and lightness.

ABOVE The axis of the pool is set at a diagonal to the house giving dynamism and individuality to the whole.

a painter's home

PREVIOUS PAGE Some decorative
teakwood carvings from Borneo
add cultural interest in the
compound garden. The guest
pavilion is in the background.

ABOVE The living area, situated in
its own freestanding pavilion,
is curiously formal with custom-
crafted sofa and divans.
Designed by the owner in wood
and leather along a somewhat
retro theme, they are accented
with mauve silk cushions. Carved
wooden panels depicting scenes
from nature hang on the walls
and other decorative items
include outsize wooden balls and
spheres crafted from tamarind
wood. The harp-shaped lamp in
stretched purple silk and metal
is designed by Doumeng.

Built in the year 2000 on a 5,300 square metre (6,340 sq yards) plot in Pereranang Canggu, this
house is an interesting example of the synthesis of fairly traditional Balinese architecture with modern
artworks, a specific colour scheme and an artist's eye. It certainly couldn't be called modern (as the
buildings are firmly rooted in Bali pavilion style); yet neither is it antique. Rather, it's a classic combo
of old and new working together.

Sandwiched between river, rice field and sea, the compound comprises several detached, thatched-
roofed pavilions all surrounding a central rectangular swimming pool. Mimicking the traditional
Bali compound design of open-sided, freestanding pavilions connected by pools, courts and temple,
the layout was designed by artist owner Pascale Doumeng with designer Yudi Atmajaya. Set in an
expansive garden with a central swimming pool, it features reflecting lily and lotus ponds, meandering
pathways and poolside loungers in addition to the various buildings.

These include one main two-storey building with master bedroom, a junior suite for the painter's
children and a working atelier; a detached pavilion for guests; a further pavilion with the generous
living/dining area; and a smaller bar/relaxation pavilion.

There are no surprises in the materials: As befits the trad Bali theme, teakwood and *bengkerai* are used in profusion along with *alang-alang* roofing and local stone. The latter includes *paras*, creamy *palimanan*, Kerobokan stone in ponds and walls, and grey andesite. Polished cement and terrazzo floors are cool underfoot, while the green, glowing stone used for the pool is entirely in keeping with the lush, land-scaped surrounds.

Where the compound does break with the traditional is in the interiors, which are noteworthy for their specific colour scheme and meticulous attention to detail. "I have tried to highlight and mix the *coté sauvage* of nature together with the calm and tranquility that spreads around by the extensive use of different tones of violet and mauve," explains Doumeng. She goes on to explain that such shades are considered the colours of harmony, and, when combined with simple architecture and certain choice pieces of furniture, give a "comforting yet magical" atmosphere. Certainly, when accentuated with the owner's extensive collection of artworks, the result is intriguing and easy on the eye.

Other notable features include careful lighting along with statuary, fountains, some rustic-modern pieces, custom-crafted retro-contemporary furniture and driftwood artifacts. The overall feeling is of well-being along with a true sense of place—in the heart of Bali's lush and exotic landscape.

ABOVE At the entrance to Chalina villa a pathway of asymmetric unpolished black terrazzo inset in a lawn of white pebbles surrounded by lily ponds leads to the living/dining pavilion on left or down to the pool area (in background). Two conical standing vases frame the view of the lower level and surrounding vegetation

LEFT The slightly raised dining area furthers the mauve theme from the living area with bucket chairs in rattan set around a table made from one piece of solid teakwood.

FAR LEFT A covered corridor on the right hand side of the entrance connects the main building and the master bedroom. Decorated with oversize conical vases that double up as water features and a series of paintings of nudes by the owner, it is both functional and aesthetic.

ABOVE The interior of the bar pavilion is dominated by some large canvasses by the artist owner: behind the bar, a duo called "Equity" and "Balance" (2004) and, on right, "Mon Boudha" (2007). On the bar top, an abstract u-shaped wood sculpture from Asmara is surrounded by a number of tribal artifacts giving an ethnic feel that is furthered by the roughly hewn table at centre, also from Asmara. An example of the artist's eye is illustrated by the primitive table being waxed and shining, to accentuate the long shiny bar top in black granite. The latter works well with the ebony finish sofa that has echoes of 1920s Charles Rennie Mackintosh Art Nouveau pieces.

LEFT Also in the bar pavilion, a large hanging lamp in front of the canvas entitled "Chalina" (2005) is from Delighting; made from resin and fabric, its inspiration came from the Ramayana story.

OPPOSITE The pool acts as the focal point for the whole compound. Surrounded by teakwood loungers and relaxation *balés*, it constitutes a typically trad-Bali scene. The owners named the compound Chalina, a mix of their two children's names, as they wanted the house to be a true family home.

LEFT The master bedroom has an outsize bed at centre; made from antique pieces of teakwood painted black, it is hung with gauzy drapes. Along with the sculpture-like trunk against the wall, in contrast to the polished teakwood floor, it is somewhat rustic. There is a walk-in open wardrobe on the mezzanine level and a low-level occasional table on rollers. On it stands a "running lovers" sculpture called "Connexion" in mixed media (2006).

ABOVE The bathroom follows the mauve theme with towels in deep purple and an over-large canvas painted by the owner called "Circle Dance". A wrought-iron standing lamp, "Antinea" by Terzani in metal and amber glass, stands next to the handmade hammered stainless steel in terrazzo tub.

organic house

Completed in 2004 by GM Architects on a wild, steeply sloping site in the Canggu area, this home is a prime example of how architecture may be merged with its surrounds in a harmonious fashion. The home almost seems to rise out of the ground in which it is anchored; volumes, terraces and pools are all sited at different levels depending on the contours and shape of the land, and all fit snugly into the existing topography. This "organic" approach is furthered by the use of 100 percent natural materials—wood shingles on roofs, wood and stone in construction, and natural materials in furniture and furnishings.

As with many GM projects, the main villa is characterized by a pair of bold, "flying" butterfly-like roofs. Insulated with ironwood shingles, one covers the owner's daughter's quarter which comprises a living/ dining area with kitchen and various terraces on the upper floor and two bedrooms with a private pool on the lower floor; the other protects the main living-relaxing mezzanine area and is part of a more articulated architectural composition made of various volumes interacting together. In this part of

the house, there is also an office and a dining area, and a kitchen and service area below. Slightly lower and off to one side, there is a further "flying" roof, beneath which is the master bedroom.

When approaching the house from the parking lot, the interaction with nature is immediately obvious. The house backs on to a forest full of mature trees and semi-wild vegetation, and in front is a lawn (landscaped artfully at a number of different levels), a lily pond and a selection of paths and steps that intersect and work with the contours of the land. One of these leads across lawn, land and water to disappear between the spot where the two roofs meet. As the house is built on a slope, access is at the upper level.

Once within the home, this relationship between the architecture and the surrounding nature becomes more obvious. There is a fluidity of transition between both inside and out, as well as between the different areas within the villa. Formal entrances have been eschewed in favour of freer boundaries: for example, an area where a roof cascades down to the ground may reveal an opening or a terrace may flow naturally out from a "room". This, in turn, encourages natural ventilation and an elemental feeling of living with, rather than separate from, the natural world.

The design of this home is clearly at the forefront of modern tropical living: the villa is sophisticated and smart, it is furnished with a designer's eye for form and function, and has all the modern conveniences needed in today's world. Yet, it also works naturally with its drop-dead gorgeous surrounds, complements the serenity of Bali's magical landscape, and invites it into the various parts of the home.

ABOVE A curved walkway in pre-cast pebblewash slabs leads from the parking area to the two entrances of the villa which are located in the central cut of the twin roofs. Wavy terraces and the swirling shape of the path are countered by the triangular roofs and a solid inclined block clad with green Indian stone (on right).

BELOW The living area comprises a dynamic space organized on different levels; the entrance is seen on left and, on right, a patio leads out to the garden and pool. Wood predominates with flooring in teakwood, a fascia surrounding the sofas in teakwood, and a black Indian slate and teak staircase. The wall in ivory *palimanan* stone serves as a suitably neutral backdrop for elegant, masterfully crafted furniture by Carlo, refined artworks from Peter Dittmar and a roughly hewn, triangular teakwood art-piece from Ideas. The "fish" lamp is also from Carlo.

LEFT A close-up view of the trefoil-like table in terrazzo on the mezzanine (seen partially obscured in photo below).

ABOVE Another view of the living area protected by GM Architects' signature roof. The console adjacent the sofa by Carlo holds a candle holder in wood and glass by Seiki Torige, while other decorative items include a mahogany root sculpture on left and a round black ironwood artwork in the far corner, both by Nishihata for Nakara.

LEFT A small platform of wood marks the entrance to the main living area. Green stone cladding on the right contrasts with a vertical trapezoid wall at the back. At the entrance a square partition composed of thin strips of grey stone contrasts in texture and colour while acting as a modern interpretation of an *aling-aling*. The wooden sculpture in front of it is by Yasukazu Nishihata for Nakara. Behind, on the console, is another art-piece in mahogany root by the same artist.

RIGHT The entrance to the living/dining area in the second section of the house features a natural yellow patterned curved wall in soft *paras* stone with a kitchen behind. Different flooring textures include wooden planks, black Indian slates with wooden insets and pebble-wash in the mezzanine.

ABOVE In the same building sits an adjacent compact mezzanine dining area featuring a sculptural dining table in *lawaan* wood and glass and chairs in *abaca*, nylon and mahogany from Deefusion. The wood-and-glass flower holder on the back console and the glass plate on the table are both by glass artist Seiki Torige. The room is further accessorised by two well-preserved antique Toraja panels from Just Jen's.

OPPOSITE A teakwood floor and steeply inclined roof in wood give character and softness to the modern furnishings in the living room. The sofa is made from resin, coconut palm cores and wood with a white glazed finish, as is the Wavy bench on right. The Rebba cube coffee table is in plywood and resin and features a "sliced termite" pattern. Sculptural vases in bamboo-skin strips, white wood and resin offset the black penshell and mirror lamps. Outside on the deck is another similar sofa, this time with a transparent finish, accompanied by a matching coffee table with decorative legs in stainless steel. All are from Deefusion.

OPPOSITE BELOW from LEFT to RIGHT Close-up view of the resin, coconut palm core and wood pattern on the outside furniture; Seike Torige glass plate; close-up of the sliced termite pattern of the coffee table.

BELOW The master bedroom, sheltered beneath an inclined roof, has teakwood floors and a cosy deck open to the jungle. Taupe and tobacco tones predominate for a restful, relaxed feeling. Disini furniture in white-washed wood and hand-woven embroidered bed linen complement the matching lamps by Senso for Disini. The two photo-digital art pieces on enamel board are by Pamela Cochrane, while the pair of horses with riders is antique.

ABOVE from LEFT to RIGHT Detail of the coconut palm and resin white glaze finish of the bench in the living room; detail of the wooden dining table stand in matte black finish; detail of the sofa pattern in the same material as the bench.

LEFT The master bedroom's triangular *bengkerai* wooden deck, supported by a v-shaped wooden structure, juts out dramatically into the surrounding garden and vegetation. A sofa-bench in white-washed tropical wood with metal legs by Disini is flanked by two antique wooden ancestor statues from Borneo.

BELOW A curved "bridge" of pink Indian slabs leads over a lily pond towards the entrance of the Van Delft residence. The angular edges of both volumes and planes in wooden shingles and stone interact with the soft curvilinear landscape design.

RIGHT TOP A curved outside staircase with large pebblewashed steps leads down to the green-tiled pool and becomes an element of the landscaping. On the left, an unusually shaped meditation *balé* looks out on to untouched tropical vegetation and the river below. Fragrant frangipani and variegated bougainvillea give a touch of colour.

RIGHT BOTTOM From below, the profile of the Van Delft villa is a combination of sharp slim inclined shingled roof planes and flat terraces and decks that jut out over the steep sloping garden. On the curved deck is a Bettina double lounger with coated iron bars and PVC weave from Deefusion.

a sensitive renovation

The Batujimbar area in Sanur is best known for the beautiful estate masterplan that was drawn up by Geoffrey Bawa in the early 1970s at the request of Australian artist Donald Friend. Unfortunately never completed, it comprised a series of Balinese pavilion-style homes in a classical Balinese garden. The estate was divided into 15 plots, each individually designed with raised living/dining pavilions with loggias and thatched roofs leading into enclosed sleeping rooms decorated with thick walls of rubble and coral. Each was set around a pool, amidst a profusion of decorative masonry and statuary, water features and tropical ornamentals.

Although only five of the original 15 were built (the other plots were developed later without adhering to Bawa's plan), Batujimbar became known throughout the tropical world for its vision of indulgent, elegant indoor-outdoor living. In his 1976 book *The Cosmic Turtle* Friend calls it one of Bawa's "architectural masterpieces". With its inspiration rooted in the 19th-century palaces at Klungkung and Amlapura, Batujimbar's design became a benchmark for tropical dream seekers the world over.

Bawa's pavilion style was copied, distilled, distorted and diluted over the ensuing decades—but it wouldn't be stretching the truth to say that his influence still lives on. For sure, yesteryear's thatch and bamboo have been replaced by glass and metal, much entirely local decoration has been substituted by hybrid East meets West products, and furniture and furnishings are far more sophisticated and stylish these days. Yet many homes island-wide still seek to emulate the enduring spirit of Bali so encapsulated by Bawa, along with a sincere respect for Balinese crafts and traditions.

This Batujimbar house is a good example of such a home. Set on one of the original 15 plots, it was renovated, expanded and updated in 2006. Two Indonesian architects from Imago Design Studio, Yulanda Fariani and Iwan Virga Sutanto, oversaw the design of two new pavilions that complemented the main building's architectural language, while French designer Isabelle Raison modernized and revamped the interiors. "In keeping with the spirit of the old Batujimbar, I tried to maximize the beauty of the garden and give a timeless feeling along with a touch of modernity," she explains.

To do this, she needed "lightness and transparency", so she used a lot of frameless glass, nearly no walls, all white paint and neutral colours with light *palimanan* stone from Java and white-washed teak. Refined wooden blinds replaced the older heavy chicks, and some innovative contemporary furniture was commissioned. The finished result is a home that respects the heritage of the past, but embraces the cleaner, all-transparent look of the present.

Would Bawa and Friend have approved? The designers sincerely hope so.

RIGHT and OPPOSITE BOTTOM The living pavilion features a central floor covered in large, lightly white-washed teakwood planks; these are surrounded by ivory *palimanan* stone tiles that extend out to the garden, thereby connecting inside with out. Transparency is maximized with extensive use of frameless glass and sliding panels, while slim wooden Venetian blinds provide protection and privacy when needed. The sectional l-shaped sofa in grey-washed rattan is from Bali Rattan; the upholstery and silk cushions, along with the *palimanan* walls, are wonderfully light. Two side lamps in silver with black shades are by Disini, while the oval-shaped coffee table in laminated bamboo from Deefusion adds texture and pattern. An antique Leti panel from Wamena Gallery with delicate carving hangs on the wall.

BELOW An unusual dining table in curved veneered wood and glass takes centre stage in the large airy pavilion. The lightweight chairs in *tinalak* or *abaca* fibre with mahogany legs are suitable for the tropics. Both are from Deefusion.

BOTTOM The living area opens out to the pool with its surrounds of ivory stone. The building at the end houses the bedroom.

OPPOSITE, LEFT and BELOW A simple palette of colours, clean lines and luxurious linens characterize this tropical-modern bedroom and bathroom. A love seat in a niche is backed by an old Balinese wood panel painted in vegetal colours. On left, sliding doors separate the room from the walk-in wardrobe behind. Semi-transparent bamboo curtains on sliding doors screen the bathroom, which is fresh, tropical and open to the outside. The textured rubble wall, newly painted white, is noteworthy. Wooden blinds and a floor in teakwood and *palimanan* stone further texturize the rooms.

artist's residence

In today's world, environmental pollution and ways to counteract or reduce it, is a subject that more and more people are taking seriously. For example, many NGOs (Non Governmental Organisations) and governments are encouraging people to include environmental impact assessments in building projects. These aim to encourage both industry and individuals to build in a sustainable manner.

Of course, there are many arguments as to what exactly sustainability is, but there is broad agreement that one of the factors contributing to a sustainable project is the absence of pollution. As such, a term increasingly bandied around these days is that of VOCs or Volatile Organic Compounds. In construction, processes involving solvents, paints or the use of chemicals often product VOCs in the form of polluting gases and vapours. This project, built on the side of a steep river valley outside Ubud, is significant in that it was constructed with materials that produce no VOCs at all. Both architect Giuseppe Verdacchi and designer Putu Eka Budi Teresna are extremely proud of this fact, as is the owner, an American artist who uses the house as her atelier home.

Built on section of committed environmentalist Linda Garland's property in Panchoran Ubud, the house sits on a ledge that juts out from the side of a gorge. It comprises two two-storey buildings connected by a central elliptical staircase. Inspired by the strong presence of the surrounding nature (trees, bamboo and river) and a desire for a type of "organic architecture", it fits snugly in its somewhat wild, overgrown setting.

Materials reflect this natural theme: The house sits on a platform of local lava stone and the base of the house is also of lava stone. The second, entrance level storey is all wood, while the roofs are shingled. The bearing structure of the ground floor is in tubular steel clad in soldered copper: copper oxidates to a nuance of brown that almost perfectly matches the colour of the wood above, but also maintains its metallic character. It is finished somewhat roughly, bent and wrapped by hand. Similarly rustic is the use of round steel structural supports also wrapped in copper: these recall the natural shapes in the vicinity and are referred to as "bamboo memory" by the designer. The ground floor uses a great deal of glass—giving an overall feeling of transparency, thus inviting the outside in.

With the master bedroom and living/dining spaces above, and the guest quarters and atelier below, the house is plastered in quicklime and ground white limestone. This, no doubt, aids with its non-VOC status—as does flooring in wood and limestone.

PREVIOUS PAGE The interior design of the home was overseen by Linda Garland who adheres to her commitment to bamboo in this project. This is exemplified by the living room's furniture, most of which is designed by Giuseppe Verdacchi using bamboo. A coffee table fashioned from ebony from Sulawesi with an andesite stone base sits in front of a large, white cotton-covered sofa. On left is an all-wood corner chest of drawers and an imaginative standing lamp composed from an old wooden plough and dried coconut leaves. Atop the chest of drawers is an attractive vase made from interwoven bamboo.

RIGHT Reconstructed white limestone slabs form the pathway to the entrance of the house, located in the wood-and-glass central elliptical volume. The second-storey materials are clearly seen here: external panels of the two buildings are in woven split bamboo with embossed copper fascia and the roofs are wood shingled.

TOP The house, as seen from the opposite bank of the river. The lower floor utilises large panes of glass, while the first storey is built from wood. The unusual central connector with staircase is topped by a soldered copper "hat" that is perforated, thereby aiding with ventilation.

ABOVE Clad almost entirely in glass with panoramic views of the surrounding jungle, this white-and-silver room is the owner's artistic sanctuary. Always resident is her pet white rabbit. Outsized tiles made of reconstructed white limestone are cool underfoot, while a silver leaf finish forms the outer layer and ceiling of the copper-clad structure. Two silver beanbags, *Sacco* by Zanotta, give a slightly 1970s retro feel; designed in 1968, they are still popular today. An antique wooden console with marble tabletop has been distressed and the legs dressed with white fabric.

RIGHT and OPPOSITE The master bedroom features a simple platform bed with hanging bamboo poles supporting a softly billowing mosquito net. The wooden floorboards have a wide cut, while the square bamboo-weave table with interwoven bamboo bowl with tuberoses furthers the overall "bamboo theme". In the background on left is a pair of sculptural chairs made from a single piece of coconut wood.

OPPOSITE The central staircase connecting the two floors of the house has an internal elliptical bearing structure made of wooden studs and an external "skin" in wood and polycarbonate. It houses a central staircase, the treads of which are inserted into the studs and splay out at ground level into a bed of white pebbles. At the top are an assembly of Balinese statuary and a statue of the Buddha placed to welcome guests.

ABOVE The entrance to the home on the top level. The wooden walkway is thoughtfully provided with small concealed lights on either side.

LEFT A slightly stark bathroom features a rigidly designed bathtub in pre-cast grey terrazzo set in a floor of extra large tiles in reconstructed white limestone. Large picture windows of bamboo and bougainvillea give the room life and colour.

a symphony of
white on white

ABOVE One of the four villas, each of
which has a generously glazed master
bedroom with stunning views over the
ocean on the first floor. The bedroom's
shape, characterized by a low-sloping
wooden shingled pitched roof, plays
well with the uneven elongated volume
beneath. On the left is an impressive
glass sculpture by Seiki Torige.

PREVIOUS PAGE The resort's communal
swimming pool seemingly juts out over
the Indian ocean. On the right, under
a manicured flat roof, is the breezy,
open-to-the-ocean bar and lounge with
beguiling vistas over the Bukit's famed
surfing beaches.

The Calyx, a four-villa boutique resort with a stunning clifftop location in southwest Bali, takes
its name from the part of a plant that supports the flower. It is intended to portray the caring
attitude of the Japanese owners. "Just as a calyx, or to use the Japanese word, the *utena*,
supports its flower, we support the guests in the resort," says the management. A large part of
that support structure comes from the richness of the resort's chosen location, the architecture
and the clean-lined interiors.

The commissioned architects were Gfab, a firm that tries to introduce energy efficiency and
sensitivity to the environment into each and every project. "As with all projects," says Gary Fell of
the firm, "the design of the Calyx was dictated by the site." In order to preserve uninterrupted
views of Dreamlands beach below and the volcanoes behind, Gfab "buried" all the buildings so
that you enter at a high level and drop down into the living spaces. The soft sandstone that was
cut from the site during excavation work was then resized and used to clad the walls, giving the
villas a creamy cool look. Pitched roofs were minimized; indeed, many are flat and covered with
either plantings or water. This has the dual purpose of further blending the buildings into the
landscape as well as adding to their thermal capacity.

Fell explains: "With plantings, the soil acts as insulation and the water roofs reflect the sun's rays off the spaces below, so all rooms are naturally cool without air conditioning despite being in the tropics. The effects are aesthetic, yet the principals behind are practical and vital." Gfab believes that in the present economic and cultural situation intelligent designers should be concerned about their carbon imprint—and all of Gfab's work explores ways of minimizing impacts.

In keeping with Gfab's usual *modus operandi*, the company oversaw the Calyx's interiors, lighting and landscaping as well. A huge Seiki Torige glass sculpture forms the centerpiece of the resort, which retains the site's indigenous gum trees. The villas are built so as to make the most of open-air living with floor-to-ceiling glass fronts, private infinity-edge pools with whirlpools and plantings instead of walls between villas. White limestone combines with wood, suede and white cotton furnishings. Floors are cool underfoot in polished and roughly-finished terrazzo. The overall feeling is sequestered, tranquil, refreshing – with a hefty dose of modernism.

Each two-bedroom villa has been named after the elements—water, fire, earth and air. We're not too sure about the fiery aspect (though perhaps that comes from being able to see both sunrise and sunset from one vista), but water, earth and air are all supremely present—the resort's water bodies, cool breezes and characteristic local *paras* stone see to that.

ABOVE A walkway with steps leads from the parking area to the villa complex at the Calyx. The walls are clad in local white *paras* limestone, while a modernist glass-and-metal structure stands above. The floor is in pebblewashed concrete.

LEFT The Calyx has Japanese owners, and this is reflected in the interior living space of the villas. Diners are offered the choice of the central *horigotatsu* table or a dining table adjacent the kitchenette, while seating is in-built. Tones are rigorously ivory and white, in furnishing, *paras*-clad walls and polished terrazzo flooring. On the wall is an artwork by Japanese artist Sumio Suzuki.

ABOVE Each villa is more or less identical with plantings used as dividers between villas.

LEFT The master bedroom is slightly warmer than the public spaces with a pleasant, balanced combination of wooden and ivory-coloured surfaces and volumes. In the background, behind a floor-to-ceiling glazed partition, is the bathroom, accessed by an outsized wooden door,.

RIGHT This detail of the *horigotatsu* table shows how flooring is patterned by geometric polished and rough finishes in the terrazzo.

made in heaven

It would be easy to think you had died and gone to heaven if you tied the knot in one of the Tirtha wedding chapels. Perched seemingly in the sky, they comprise two series of buildings set on a cliff amidst watery surrounds. Hovering above the Indian ocean as if in a bubble, they contain all the ingredients of a perfect wedding day.

The brainchild of a Japanese entrepreneur, Tirtha Uluwatu and the later addition of Tirtha Luhur are an inspired adjunct to Bali's touristic scene. Situated on a stunning clifftop location near one of the island's most revered temples, they offer a bespoke wedding service for bridal couples. They are also architecturally unique.

Both are designed by Glenn Parker, of Bali-based Glenn Parker Architects. Landscaping, a central tenet of the project with pools within pools, statuary and lush ornamentals, is by Made Wijaya and interiors by Ratina Moegiono of PT Alindi Kyati Praya. The 15-pavilion Tirtha Uluwatu came first in 2003, and was followed by the three-bedroom Tirtha Luhur villa a couple of years later.

A sense of progression from traditional to modern is fundamental to Tirtha Uluwatu's design. The bridal party enters via a romantic Balinese gate where ivory *palimanan* stone predominates, then proceeds through a series of courtyards, pavilions, paths and pools to culminate in the heart of the resort—the clifftop chapel. This is an A-line structure with white steel frames, panels of suspended tempered glass and a triangular Teflon roof, seemingly floating above a large reflecting pool and framed by sea, horizon and sky. Described by Parker as something like a "folly" or "a lantern floating on a pond," it is undeniably dramatic. Nonetheless, says Parker, it is anchored in a contemporary Asian vernacular that responds to climate, topography, available materials, and the social and cultural issues present in its location.

Tirtha Luhur adds to the Tirtha concept with another air-conditioned wedding chapel, this time with the added bonus of accommodations. Set adjacent its sister property, it comprises an exclusive three-bedroom luxury villa with indoor and outdoor dining options, swimming pool, *balé* and bar. Quality is key here: interiors boast Prada teak wood finishing, wall panels and soft furnishings in Jim Thompson silk fabrics and super-soft leather sofas. Spread over 3,000 square metres (3,590 sq yards) it also has views to die for.

Both projects display a modernist sensibility, but retain elements of Balinese culture and tradition. They offer a service, but also stand alone as interesting examples of contemporary-tropical architecture. Bravo to those who have the time and the money to treat themselves—and to owner and architect alike.

PREVIOUS PAGE Comprising a walk-through antechamber as well as the larger atrium building itself, Glenn Parker's Tirtha Uluwatu wedding chapel is characterized by an ethereal quality of lightness and romance. Expansive water bodies and views of the Indian ocean add to this otherworldly effect; it is interesting to note that Tirtha translates as "holy water".

ABOVE An extensive use of ivory *palimanan* stone on floors and walls, along with *alang-alang* roofs and traditional statuary gives the entrance to Tirtha Uluwatu a traditional, yet clean-lined, Balinese-Javanese air.

RIGHT The sharp verticality of the all-white architectural lines adds emotion at the entrance of the wedding chapel.

OPPOSITE TOP At the entrance, a stele-like metallic central stand with a tropical flower arrangement rises from the smooth ivory *palimanan* floor.

LEFT From above, Tirtha Uluwatu's roofs resemble sails; surrounded by frangipani, palms and reflecting pools, they project an ethereal quality.

BELOW The master bedroom in Tirtha Luhur is tactile and romantic with interiors by Ratina Moegiono. Geometric panels behind the bed are covered in Jim Thompson silk, while bed linen is high-quality Egyptian cotton.

OPPOSITE BOTTOM The open-to-the-sky master bathroom is a vision of cream and ivory tones. Composed from *palimanan* stone, it reflects the high-style indulgence of the whole complex.

ABOVE A close-up view of the Tirtha Luhur chapel shows its structure clearly. Composed of V-shaped columns in steel with horizontal beams between the columns in white-painted steel, it has a suspended ceiling with "scales" plastered in white. The lights between these scales produce decorative drama, while flooring is in bamboo and white *palimanan* stone.

BELOW The villa and chapel are flanked by a 22-metre (72-ft) swimming pool that stretches out towards the ocean beyond.

RIGHT Balinese and Javanese palaces were traditionally built around copious water bodies, with meandering paths and reflecting pools. Tirtha Uluwatu's design inspiration is firmly rooted in this vernacular, although it is strictly 21st century in style.

ABOVE The spacious air-conditioned Tirtha Luhur wedding pavilion allows for seating of up to 100 guests; on the right is the main dining pavilion with spectacular views across the Indian ocean.

RIGHT A general view of Tirtha Uluwatu at dusk. The unique chapel and wide guest pavilion on the right are surrounded by an expansive reflecting pool.

glass and bamboo
reinterpreted

As we begin to pay more than lip service to sustainability in daily life, so too do architects and interior designers in their work. Many are beginning to explore avenues that impact less on the environment, use ecologically friendly materials and reflect the bio-diversity of a locale. One interesting example, built in Bali in 2004, is a restaurant adjacent the spa and villa complex of Kayumanis Nusa Dua.

Designed and constructed by Indonesian architect Budi Pradono, the restaurant is based on the idea of a *taring* or *tetaring*. This is a Balinese structure that is traditionally built as a temporary ceremonial pavilion. Comprising three parts—two lightweight pavilions in bamboo and glass and one heavyweight structure entirely built from clay—the restaurant draws skillfully on vernacular materials.

The entrance lobby is situated in the solid rammed earth structure. A long, thin, impermeable building, it separates the open-to-the-public restaurant from the privacy of the villa complex. Attached are two semi-transparent pavilions that house the reception, dining and drinking spaces. The bearing structure is in steel clad all in bamboo—as an external skin, as an internal skin for the ceiling, and as a shading device on sliding vertical panels on the sides. The result is a simple but refined building that is at once contemporary and tropical.

"In this project I wanted to bring bamboo into modern architecture by combining it with other elements such as acrylic, polycarbonate, glass and steel," explains Pradono. "And to make the bamboo look more modern, I used bamboo pins as joints instead of rope." He goes on to add that bamboo offers an ecologically viable alternative to timber for construction as it is extremely fast growing, and unlike with other trees, bamboo plants are not killed by harvesting thereby avoiding erosion problems. Also, by utilising clay as do some of the Balinese in their homes, Pradono was able to achieve a conceptual whole that juxtaposed light with heavy, fragmented with solid.

"The massive material I selected is clay, while the fragmented one is bamboo," he explains. The rustic, uneven textures of both are combined with various irregularities in the space planning, so that an architectural rhythm is achieved. In addition, natural light filters through seemingly floating ceilings and walls and breezes are ever-present as the whole complex is built around a reflecting pool.

PREVIOUS PAGE The reception area as seen from within. A roughly-hewn single piece of wood forms a dramatic counter, while the spiralling wood decorative piece accentuates the architect's use of indigenous materials.

ABOVE An interior perspective of the clay entrance corridor: The ceiling is glazed with a floating bamboo screen beneath; the bamboo allows light to filter through while simultaneously offering protection and shade from the sun.

RIGHT Built from local clay, this massive volume acts as a dividing element between the restaurant (on left) and the neighbouring villas (on right). Its inspiration comes from an interpretation of the low-tech buildings from the Bali Aga era.

ABOVE A relaxing corner on the first floor of the two-storey pavilion features glass walls, black marble floors, external screens of bamboo and two modern classic black leather Barcelona Chairs by Mies van der Rohe.

OPPOSITE TOP Dressed in white, this internal view of the restaurant highlights the polished marble floor, glass walls and bamboo features. With interior design by Endramukti Design Associates, the total transparency of the space accentuates the feeling of floating above the surrounding water.

OPPOSITE BOTTOM A detail of the external shadowing bamboo panels of the two-storey lightweight pavilion illustrates the interesting structural concept of the restaurant.

188

BELOW The three different volumes of the Kayumanis restaurant are seen from this angle: On the left is the single-storey restaurant, at centre the two-storey building that houses the reception area, drinking and relaxing areas and open-air restaurant with deck, and on the right the massive clay building with ramp.

BOTTOM The entrance to the restaurant reception area stands between two vertical panels of bamboo that are connected together with Plexiglass horizontal bars. Walls of glass work with white sandstone steps, a lawn of grey pebbles inside and out, and black polished marble within.

ABOVE A single-storey lightweight pavilion seemingly floats over a large reflecting pool that meanders through the whole complex. The over-water walkway and fountain provide a tranquil setting for the deck in polished absolute black marble that juts out over the pool. Landscaping by Karl Princic Design includes a variety of water plants.

RIGHT Another view of the same building illustrates how a false bamboo ceiling and semi-transparent "walls" work within the larger whole.

on the cliff's edge

PREVIOUS PAGE One side of the house is surrounded by hardwood decking and a long slim pool over two levels. Green/grey stones and tiles are used to reflect the different colours of the ocean and sky.

ABOVE The entrance leads directly into an open-plan living/dining area that is furnished simply allowing the eye to take in superb ocean views. The solid teak furniture was handmade by local artist Aulia who also works with wood and has designed many artworks for the owners' home in New Zealand. The large bowl on the coffee table is a housewarming gift; likewise the primitive statue from Sumatra on the bench. The Buddha head on the wall was bought in Seminyak; the wall design was organized to suit it.

LEFT A slightly inclined copper roof casts shade over a projecting double-height balé that is one of the owner's favourite places for relaxing.

Situated on a long, narrow rectangular strip of land on the Bukit peninsula, the design of this holiday home was largely dictated by the confines of the site. There wasn't a lot of room to play around with (1,148 square metres; 1,370 square yards), so the architect decided to concentrate on the cliff top location and its variety of moods and colours instead. Depending on the time of the day and the state of the weather, the natural environment changes dramatically here. Hues of seaweed green, sandy shades of taupe and beige, ocean emeralds and deep blues are all utilised in one way or another.

The result is a simple, functional two-storey home with an iconic pool on stilts. According to Walter Wagner of Bali-based architects Habitat5 the pool "almost resembles a boat on dry dock". Seemingly floating with its prow facing out to sea, it is the central focus of the house. Built from concrete, *batu hijau* green stone tiles and Himalayan green slate, it is statement making in both shape and colour. It even has cute "portholes" on its "hull"! And since it is on two levels, with water overflowing from the upper lap pool to the lower paddling pools, the sound of water is ever present.

All other structures radiate out from the pool: the functional two-storey home, with living quarters and master suite above, guest quarters below, a long balustraded walkway leading to a *balé*, and the double-height *balé* itself. The latter is also an interesting feature, as it projects out to the cliff from the pool end and provides a secluded breezy relaxation area with panoramic views. Both structure and deck are built from *benkerai* wood, while the roof is in copper. Wagner specifically chose copper because it ages fast, and when exposed to air, oxidises into a creamy green colour. He felt this matched the seaweed carpets far below.

The interiors were mainly designed by the New Zealand couple who own the home. Their desire for function and simplicity in the architecture is carried through in the somewhat masculine style of furniture and furnishings. In the living/dining area, severe grey pillars clad in *batu candi* stone and *merbau* wood floors form the backdrop for some clean-lined, custom-crafted furniture. Elsewhere, on the outdoor terrace and in the clean-lined bedrooms and bathrooms, materials predominate: excavated limestone cut to size, acid washed marble, polished and unpolished black granite, and *merbau* and *bengkerai* woods. Using a neutral palette of creams, greys and whites allows the natural textures and colours of these mostly locally-sourced materials to shine through.

The owner sums up: "We are very happy with the final result. It's a very easy house to live in and, of course, the view is spectacular."

ABOVE Shades of grey: The master bedroom has a distinctly urban vibe, with clean lines, pristine linens and a neutral colour scheme. The angular bed and console are softened with floaty drapes.

LEFT TOP A corner of the lower deck houses an open bed for massages: Unusually it sports some colour in this rather monochromatic décor scheme.

LEFT BOTTOM Masculinity is the theme in this pared down master bathroom. Granite, marble and glass give a feeling of solidity and definition; decorative detail is minimal.

ABOVE The home, with pool on stilts running the length of one side and long walkway with double-height balé, was designed for functionality and to accommodate the narrow confines of the site. Perched on the Bukit cliff top, it is made from reinforced concrete with hardwood deck surrounds and an ironwood shingle roof.

RIGHT Adjacent the living room is an outdoor relaxation area that hugs one perimeter wall. A series of lifesize figures, designed by the architect and realized by students at the BMC Polytechnic in Denpasar, line the wall.

OPPOSITE The views over the ocean are the main focus in the open-plan dining area where distressed wood and rugged stone columns provide textural detail.

RIGHT and BELOW A variety of views of pool, decks and house show how materials are important in this somewhat cramped site: The lower deck in wood contrasts with concrete pool and supports; the wooden *balé* and walkway is softened with upholstery; and water provides a cooling element throughout.

a club for
all seasons

PREVIOUS PAGE A view of the internal courtyard at night across the pool to the massive gym and spa structure; it rises up through the building and then splays out, giving a feeling of bulk and mass. Just visible is the restaurant's Japanese-inspired screen in sandblasted black glass. During the day it acts like a reflective mirror; at night it is back-lit and resembles a *shoji* screen.

ABOVE The reception area of the spa is restful and quiet. A table by Isamu Noguchi is flanked by an oversized couch and armchairs designed by Rob Sample. A 300-year-old frangipani tree reaches for the sky behind: The purpose-built metal grill allows light to filter through.

This innovative recreational complex—containing a restaurant, bar, art gallery, swimming pool, gym and spa—is an unusual addition to Bali's architectural scene. Devoid of ocean or rice field views and without easy access, it could have sunk without a trace. But because of its architectural distinction, it has made people sit up and take notice.

Described by the club's interior designer Rob Sample as "like an ocean liner—imposing from the outside, comfortable and welcoming on the inside," the structure is housed behind a 180-metre (590-ft) long sculptural screen composed of concrete, resin and fiberglass set in reinforced steel. Inspired by the Austrian sculptor Erwin Hauer, the screen gives a hard, austere exterior—thereby heightening the element of surprise one feels on entering the considerably softer, more refined, tactile interior.

Owned by Saxon Looker, a property developer from Sydney, the Sentosa Club was completed in 2007. Situated in the Petitenget beach area adjacent the Oberoi, it was designed to serve villa owners and guests at Looker's up-market Sentosa Villas round the corner. However, the complex is also open to the general public, and there is no doubt that since its opening it has garnered a considerable following.

Designed by Putu Semara, the Club is housed within an elongated L-shaped building centered round an internal garden courtyard and pool. For the most part eschewing air-conditioning for natural ventilation, the screen allows light and air to pass in from the outside. The restaurant, bar and relaxing lounge are on the ground floor, whilst the spa and gym are housed in a circular structure that flares out from the centre. The main material for construction is local *batu kali*, a stone that is generally used for foundations. Other materials are no less robust: polished concrete with glass expansion joints for floors; off-cuts of locally available *snokoling* wood for walls, ceilings and custom-crafted furniture; and *bengkerai* wood for external wooden battens and decks.

A 35-metre (115-ft) natural rock pool and sundeck are central to the Club's activity, while a rooftop wedding pavilion is a further bonus. Landscaping is an important part of the whole: Tropical ornamentals grow in profusion and a series of giant frangipani trees ranging from 150 to 300 years old are liberally planted both indoors and out. All in all, the complex offers a cooling, shady oasis for holidaymakers—and the unusual design is the icing on the cake.

TOP RIGHT The entrance to the Sentosa Club is via a round wooden clad building set on *batu kali* stone piles; its volume interplays imaginatively with a curved 5-m high x 180-m long (16 ft x 590 ft) sculptural screen. The external screen cladding is made from some 5,000 breeze blocks of GRC, a product often used as a substrata for kitchen floors. Softening is to be had in the profusion of trees and greenery.

LEFT The deck surrounding the pool is dotted with trees and natural boulders. The Kei Aloha daybeds, with strong sculptural lines, and chess piece side tables, were designed by Rob Sample.

BELOW A long banquette with footbaths sits in front of a mirrored divider in the spa. River pebbles, grey concrete flooring and indoor plants give the space a contemporary yet tropical feel.

RIGHT Counter-levered polished concrete stairs sweeping down from a 9-m (30-ft) full height mirrored wall lead to the second level of the spa.

OPPOSITE TOP The art gallery features walls and a ceiling composed of horizontal wooden strips with light entering through the external concrete screen enveloping the building. The solid teak chain sculpture is by Japanese artist Yasukazu Nishihata for Nakara. The hanging bone sculpture by London-based German artist Eva Menz is made from 2,500 pieces of cow bone; below it is a black mirror central counter. The surfing images are by Australian photographer Eugene Tan.

OPPOSITE BOTTOM One of the tables in the restaurant in foreground; a banquette clad in black mirror and couches behind. Restaurant upholstery is the same as that in the bar, as are the birdcage lights. The sculptured concrete screen allows diffused light and breeze to enter from outside.

BELOW A seating area in the communal lounge features a large sofa, club chairs, a Noguchi table and striking stainless steel sculpture by Bali-based metal artist Chen.

ABOVE An open-to-the-air relaxing area leads out to the pool. The grey concrete floor and dark brown wooden ceiling are connected by strong stone-clad elements. All furnishings—indoors and out—are designed by Rob Sample.

RIGHT This view of the Sentosa Club entrance at night shows how landscaping is integral to the overall theme. A rooftop garden, a stand of decorative grasses, and ancient frangipani trees are all clearly illuminated here.

ABOVE and BELOW The Luxe bar features a 25-m (82-ft) black mirrored bar top that doubles up as a communal eating table. Bar stools are designed by Rob Sample with a custom-designed cherry blossom print. The flower box is composed of the same wood as the furniture and ceiling cladding. The *shoji* screen is crafted from sandblasted black glass; it reflects like a mirror during the daytime, inviting the pool and landscaping in, then is back-lit at night. Locally made wooden birdcages from the market house lights that are hung haphazardly from the ceiling.

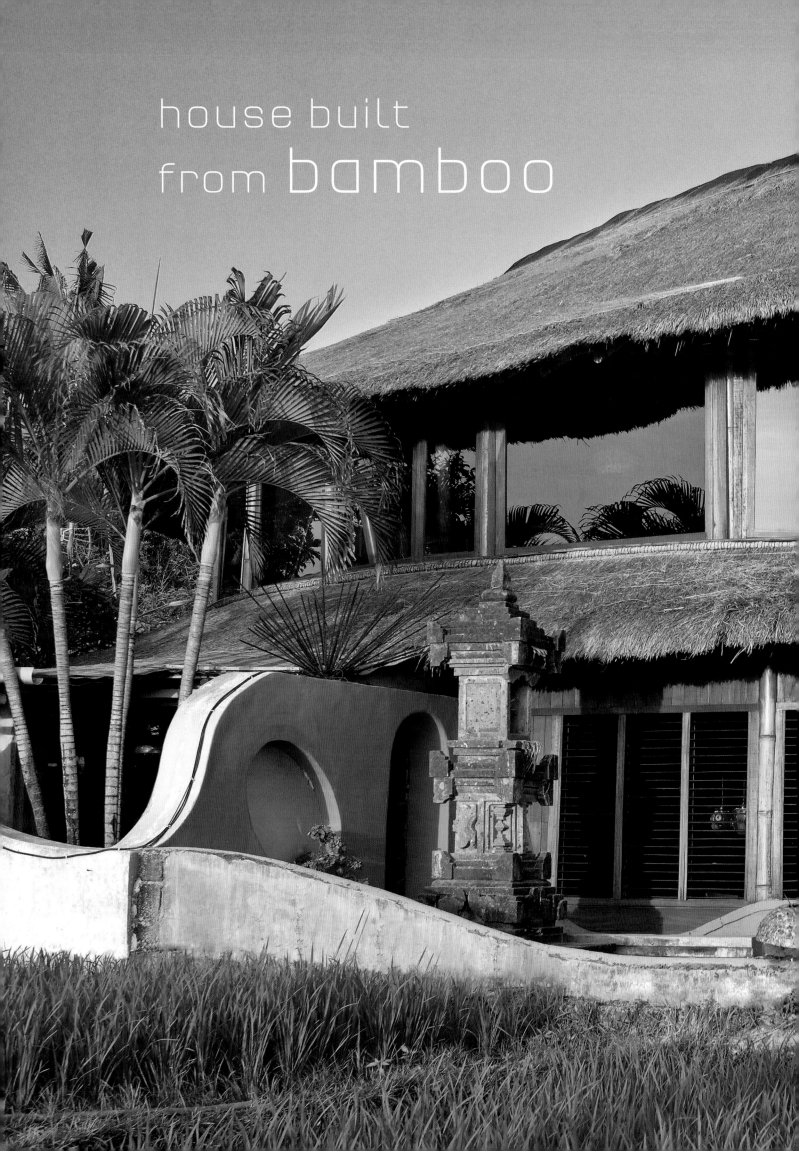

house built from bamboo

PREVIOUS PAGE The compact volume of the two-storey main house sports a roof of *alang-alang* thatch, the curved shape of which is inspired by some of the traditional architectural forms of the Indonesian archipelago. The supporting structure is entirely made of bamboo.

ABOVE This view of the relaxed, open-plan ground floor of Puri Sejuk admirably illustrates how the bearing structure of the house is entirely composed from bamboo. On left is the dining area with the kitchen behind the white wall, at centre a bar area behind two bamboo pillars at back, and a comfy living area is sited in the foreground. The curvaceous sofa in black leather was designed by the owner, while the round coffee table inset with pebbles is by Tarita Furniture. Floors are also free form, in coloured *terrazzo* with insertions of glass chips.

OPPOSITE The cosy relaxation room adjacent the master bedroom features contrasting square and triangular planes, some antique Javanese flower-patterned furnishing and decidedly curvy contemporary furniture pieces. The "Orangish" console and "Shanghai" stool in fiberglass structure with an inlay of crushed bamboo are by Tarita.

Built from 2000 to 2003 for Italian businessman, Kiko A Croserio, this villa is notable for its extensive use of bamboo in the construction. The overall feeling is rustic and unrefined, in keeping with the characteristics of the materials used. These include bamboo for poles, beams and the vital structure, pressed clay and mud for walls, wood and terrazzo for floors, and natural pebbles and stones in the outside areas. Wherever you look, you catch a glimpse of bamboo in some form or other: it gives the house a very particular character, illustrating how one of Indonesia's most vital traditional materials has been reinterpreted into a new and unusual form.

The owner enlisted the expertise of Ubud-based painter Wolfgang Widmoser to design and construct the basic house, but completed the project's landscaping and interior design himself. Widmoser, influenced by the architect Frei Otto, has a long-standing fascination with bamboo and was keen to produce something a little out of the ordinary. The situation helped too: Sited on a 2,500-square-metre (2,990-sq-yard) plot of land that slopes gently down to the beach in an entirely rural setting near Tanah Lot and the village of Seseh, the house is blessed with an abundance of Bali's natural beauty.

The fishing village of Seseh is one of only a handful of old Balinese villages that sits right on the Indian ocean. Traditional Balinese belief systems hold that the sea is full of dangerous spirits, so villages tend to be sited further inland. This one, protected by a powerful temple, is an exception. Croserio was drawn to it for this reason.

Attracted by both site and spirit, he felt emboldened to realize a "vision of living embraced by the elements of Mother Nature" using earth (the rice fields), water (the ocean and waterfall), air (the sea breezes) and fire (the volcanoes behind). He coupled these with natural materials, curvy forms and the strong spiritual presence of the neighbouring temple—and called his home *puri sejuk* or "cool palace".

The property comprises the main "bamboo house" and a detached guest pavilion set around a free-form, organic swimming pool with views through palm groves to the ocean beyond. Living is relaxed and easy in the main house where a predominantly open plan layout allows the lounging, eating, drinking and cooking spaces to flow freely from one to the other. Above, there is a master bedroom and adjoining relaxation area. All are decorated in a simple, informal, unpretentious style that suits the occupants, who come mainly from the island's holiday rental market.

OPPOSITE A somewhat retro effect is achieved in the dining area that continues the house's curvaceous theme. A white plastered wall with asymmetric serving hatch and tapering wooden shelf separates the area from the kitchen behind. The glass-and-wood oval table and '50s style chairs were chosen by the owner, while the hanging lamps are from Bikin Kibin.

ABOVE An unusual curvaceous bamboo platform forms the basis for the master bed base, where flowing mosquito drapes work well with contemporary furniture and textiles. The two fiberglass armchairs dressed with seagrass are by Tarita Furniture, while lamps are from Warisan Lighting. The bedcover and cushions, featuring bold circles and blocks, are from Disini.

LEFT Curvy forms are followed from the house into the garden, where the pool meanders around a grass lawn.

LEFT, TOP and BOTTOM The free-form swimming pool, surounded by tall palm trees, frangipani and pandanus features a small "island" and a bronze-and-metal sculpture, hand crafted locally.

RIGHT A rotund terracotta-coloured detached cottage with *alang-alang* roof houses a guest bedroom and en-suite bathroom. Somewhat tribal in style, it is connected to the main building by the pathway on left. The white, red and black pattern of the path is inspired by Australian aboriginal designs.

BELOW An outside dining area with asymmetric bamboo canopy is a super spot for al fresco dining as it has views over the pool and to the ocean beyond. During the day, the bamboo poles may be covered with fabric for shade; the refectory-like wooden dining table with benches is somewhat austere.

references

ASMARA
asmara_furniture06@yahoo.com
Jl Raya Kerobokan
Kerobokan Bali
tel: +62 361 8516830

AUDRITO VALENTINA
info@pianeta-sudest.com
http://www.pianeta-sudest.com

BALI RATTAN
Jl by Pass Ngurah Rai Sanur 47
Denpasar Bali
Tel: +62 361 738308
http://www.balirattan.net

BIKIN KIBIN
Art of Living
Jl Anoman 37
Ubud Bali

CARLO
Jl Danau Poso 22
Sanur 80228 Bali
tel: +62 361 738308
info@carloshowroom.com
http://www.carloshowroom.com

CAZENAVE ANDRE ATELIER
Tel +62 361 738308
http://www.roland-jamois.com

CHEN
Jl Gunung Salak Utara 98
Kerobokan Kuta Bali
tel: +62 361 7421970
chen@chenergy.biz

CHEONG YEW KWAN
Area Design
area@indo.net.id

COCHRANE PAMELA
Design Crop
Jl Raya Basangkasa 88A

Seminyak Bali
designcrop@yahoo.com

COCOON
cocoon@idola.net.id

D'ALESSANDRO LUCA
tel: +62 81805369749
valmaruk@yahoo.com

DEEFUSION
Jl Laksmana (Oberoi) 117X,
Seminyak 80361 Bali
tel +62 361 738308
marketing@deefusion.com
http://www.deefusion.com

DELIGHTING
Jl Gatot Subroto Barat #99
Kerobokan Kuta Bali
tel: +62 361 412194
http://www.de-lighting.com

DE SOUZA ETIENNE
etienne@indosat.net.id

DISINI
Dominique Seguin
Jl Raya Seminyak 6–8,
Basangkasa Kuta Bali
disini_bali@yahoo.com

DITTMAR PETER
Studios in Bali, Sydney, Munich
dittmart@hotmail.com
http://www.dittmart.com

DOUMENG PASCALE
artuition@pascaledoumeng.com
http://www.pascaledoumeng.com

ENDRAMUKTI DESIGN ASSOCIATES
Jl Margorejo Indah XX/D-03
Surabaya, Bali
tel: +62 31 8472924

references *continued*

FRANCIONE GIANNI
giannfr@tin.it

GARLAND LINDA
http://www.lindagarland.com

GAYA FUSION CERAMICS
marcello@gayafusion.com

GFAB ARCHITECTS
gfab@gfabarchitects.com
http://www.gfabarchitects.com

GM ARCHITECTS
gmarc@tiscalinet.it
gmarch@indo.net.id

HISHEM FURNITURE
Jl Sunset Road 18X
Denpasar Bali
Tel: +62 361 755436
info@hishem.com
http://www.hishem.com

HUTCHESON ANGUS
http://www.angoworld.com

IDEAS
Sunset Road 88B
Kuta Bali
tel: +62 361 731753
info@ideasbali.com
http://www.ideasbali.com

INGLIS KIM
http://www.kiminglis.com

IMAGO DESIGN STUDIO
imagostudio@dps.centrin.net.id

JUST JEN'S
Jl Sunset 18, Seminyak Bali
tel: +62 361 738800
justjens@indosat.net.id

KAWANA MASANO
irieeyes@pacific.net.sg

LANDI ALESSANDRO
alessandro@landi-designs.com

LE MARC
Radiant shop:
Jl. Raya Seminyak 4A
Seminyak Kuta
tel: +62 361 737085
marcle@dps.centrin.net.id

LEE ARMALI
armalilee@yahoo.com

LIGHTCOM
Komplex Pertokoan Kuta Gallery
Jl Patih Jelantik
Kuta Bali
tel: +62 361 769245
http://www.light-com.net

LOMBARDI DAVID
http://www.fullondesign-lombardi.com

MATIN ANDRA
Jl Manyar I
blok O-2 No 37
Sektor I Bintaro Jaya
Jakarta 12330 Indonesia
Andra168@cbn.net.id

MENZ EVA
http://www.evamenz.com

MOEGIONO RATINA
PT Alindi Kyati Praya
tel: +62 361 265311
alindi@indosat.net.id

NISHIHATA YASUKAZU
Nakara
Jl ByPass Sunset Road
Seminyak Kuta Bali
tel: +62 361 737101
nakarabali@indo.net.id

OLD JAVA
http://www.oldjava.com

references *continued*

PARKER GLENN
Glenn Parker Architecture and Interiors
(GPAI)
gpai@indosat.net.id

PRADONO BUDI
Budipradono Architects
http://www.budipradono.com

PRINCIC KARL W
PT Intaran Design
Jln Batur Sari #47 Intaran Bali
tel: +62 361 286462

RAISON ISABELLE
iraison@deefusion.com

SAMPLE ROB
Sample concept architecture design
www.samplecad.com

SARA YOKA
PT. Bale Legend
bale@dps.centrin.net.id

SCIASCIA FILIPPO
sciascia72@hotmail.com

SEMARA PUTU
ESA International
Esarsitek@dps.centrin.net.id
www.esarsitek.com

SENSO
PT Bali Trend Produs
Jl Tangkuban Perahu no 1 Kerobokan Bali
tel: +62 361 736 461
roberto@trendbali.com

SIRAIT PINTOR
http://www.pintorsirait.com

SUZUKI SUMIO
sumio@indo.net.id

TAN EUGENE
uge@aquabumps.com
http://www.aquabumps.com

TARITA
Jl Padang Luwih 100X
Kerobokan Kuta Bali
tel: +62 361 426344
http://www.taritafurniture.com

TERZANI
http://www.terzani.com
http://www.dmlight.com

TORIGE SEIKI
Galeri EsokLusa
Jl Raya Basangkasa 47
Seminyak Kuta Bali
http://www.esoklusa.com

TROPICAL BUILDINGS
http://www.tropicalbuildings.com

TROPLAND STUDIO
tropland@tropland.com
http://www.tropland.com

VERDACCHI GIUSEPPE
gvbali@indosat.net.id

WAGNER WALTER
Habitat5
habitat5@indosat.net.id
http://www.habitat5.com

WAMENA GALLERY
Jl Mertanadi Sunset Road 10b
Seminyak Kuta Bali
sliman@wamena-gallery.com

WARISAN
Jl Raya Padang Luwih 198
Dalung Kuta Bali
Tel: +62 361 421752
http://www.warisan.com

WIDMOSER WOLFGANG
http://www.ubud.com/wolfgangwidmoser

WIJAYA MADE
http://www.ptwijaya.com

About Tuttle
"Books to Span the East and West"

Our core mission at Tuttle Publishing is to create books which bring people together one page at a time. Tuttle was founded in 1832 in the small New England town of Rutland, Vermont (USA). Our fundamental values remain as strong today as they were then—to publish best-in-class books informing the English-speaking world about the countries and peoples of Asia. The world has become a smaller place today and Asia's economic, cultural and political influence has expanded, yet the need for meaningful dialogue and information about this diverse region has never been greater. Since 1948, Tuttle has been a leader in publishing books on the cultures, arts, cuisines, languages and literatures of Asia. Our authors and photographers have won numerous awards and Tuttle has published thousands of books on subjects ranging from martial arts to paper crafts. We welcome you to explore the wealth of information available on Asia at **www.tuttlepublishing.com.**